# GRILL BY THE BOOK

# Steaks, Chops and Burgers

By the Editors of Sunset Books

with special contributions by

Jerry Anne Di Vecchio
and
Betty Hughes

Sunset Publishing Corporation
Menlo Park, California

**President & Publisher:**
Susan J. Maruyama

**Director, Sales & Marketing:**
Richard A. Smeby

**Director, New Business:**
Kenneth Winchester

**Editorial Director:**
Bob Doyle

**Marketing & Creative Services Manager:**
Guy C. Joy

**Production Director:**
Lory Day

EDITORIAL STAFF FOR STEAKS,
CHOPS AND BURGERS

**Coordinating Editor:**
Lynne Gilberg

**Research & Text:**
Paula Smith Freschet

**Consulting Editor:**
Betty Hughes, Director, Consumer Affairs,
Weber-Stephen Products Co.

**Contributing Editors:**
Sandra Cameron
Barbara Sause
Cynthia Scheer

**Copy Editor:**
Fran Feldman

**Editorial Assistant:**
Jody Mitori

**Photography:**
Chris Shorten

**Food Stylists:**
Heidi Gintner
Susan Massey
Dianne Torrie
Sue White

**Food Styling Assistant:**
Andrea Lucich

**Prop Stylist:**
Laura Ferguson

**Design:**
Don Komai, Watermark Design

**Page Layout:**
Dayna Goforth

**Recipe Testers:**
Susan Block
Dorothy Decker
Barbara Gobar
Aileen Russell
Jean Strain
Linda Tebben

SUNSET PUBLISHING CORPORATION

**Chairman:**
Jim Nelson

**President & Chief Executive Officer:**
Stephen J. Seabolt

**Chief Financial Officer:**
James E. Mitchell

**Publisher, Sunset Magazine:**
Anthony P. Glaves

**Director of Finance:**
Larry Diamond

**Circulation Director:**
Robert I. Gursha

**Vice President, Manufacturing:**
Lorinda Reichert

**Editor, Sunset Magazine:**
William Marken

**Senior Editor, Food & Entertaining:**
Jerry Anne Di Vecchio

The kettle grill configuration is a registered trademark of WEBER-STEPHEN PRODUCTS CO.

The GENESIS®, PERFORMER®, SMOKEY JOE®, and GO ANYWHERE® grill configurations are trademarks of WEBER-STEPHEN PRODUCTS CO.

For more information on *Grill by the Book* or any other Sunset book, call (800) 634-3095. For special sales, bulk order and premium sales information, call Sunset Custom Publishing & Special Sales at (415) 324-5547.

First Edition. January 1996.
Copyright © 1996 Sunset Publishing Corporation, Menlo Park, CA 94025 and Weber-Stephen Products Co., Palatine, IL 60067. All rights reserved, including the right of reproduction in whole or part in any form.
Sunset ISBN 0-376-02004-0.
Weber ISBN 0-376-02000-8.
Library of Congress Catalog Card Number: 95-072057.
Printed in the United States.

## A word about our nutritional data

For our recipes, we provide a nutritional analysis stating calorie count; percentage of calories from fat; grams of total fat and saturated fat; milligrams of cholesterol and sodium; grams of carbohydrates, fiber, and protein; and milligrams of calcium and iron. Generally, the analysis applies to a single serving, based on the number of servings given for each recipe and the amount of each ingredient. If a range is given for the number of servings and/or the amount of an ingredient, the analysis is based on the average of the figures given.

The nutritional analysis does not include optional ingredients or those for which no specific amount is stated. If an ingredient is listed with a substitution, the information was calculated using the first choice.

# Contents

## The Art of Grilling

## Recipes

## Index

## Special Features

# The Art of Grilling

Some folks say opposites attract, and I suppose that's how it was when Weber met Sunset. Weber is a Chicago-area company with a long tradition of forming steel into very durable barbecue grills. Sunset is a San Francisco-area company with a long tradition of forming words and photographs into informative and entertaining publications.

Weber's roots are in the Midwest, and I guess that means we really appreciate a good, thick steak and meaty ribs from the heartland. Sunset's roots are in California, where fresh Pacific seafood and an almost infinite variety of vegetables abound.

Now, even if opposites attract they must have something in common for a long-term relationship to develop.

You see, at Weber we believe you ought to buy one of our products and be pleasantly surprised that it exceeds your expectations. Sunset thinks the same way. When they write a recipe, the amount of testing they do to make sure it'll come out just so is mind-boggling.

About a year ago, Weber decided to produce a series of cookbooks to help backyard chefs have more fun with their grills. Sunset was considering a similar project. So, when we shared our mutual desire to write a series of simply great barbecue cookbooks, we decided we could make them even better if we formed a partnership.

We believe that this terrific cookbook will help you have fun with your grill, but if you have any suggestions for improvements, simply give us a call at the following number: (800) 446-1071. Your comments will help us get better at what we do, and we want to make sure you're totally satisfied with our products.

*Mike Kempster*

Michael Kempster, Sr.
Executive Vice President
Weber-Stephen Products Co.

# A Range of Grill Options

Today's Weber® Grills come in a range of sizes, models, and prices, that offer backyard chefs a myriad of options. Before you purchase a grill, however, it's important to consider your cooking objectives. The grills described below offer a variety of convenient features that may be important to you.

No matter which Weber® model you choose, however, it's going to be a covered grill. The lid gives you the flexibility of using either the Direct or Indirect Methods of cooking. It also allows you to utilize more heat, reduces the amount of cooking time, and virtually eliminates flare-ups.

## Weber® One-Touch® Charcoal Kettle

With the Weber® One-Touch® Kettle, one lever opens the vents to create the natural convection heat that helps seal in juices and flavor. The same lever also simplifies ash removal. Flip-up sides on the hinged cooking grate make it easy to add charcoal briquets while food cooks.

The kettle is available in two diameters: 18½ inches (47 cm) or 22½ inches (57 cm). Both offer plenty of cooking space.

## Weber® Performer® Grill with Touch-N-Go™ Gas Ignition System

The ultimate ease in charcoal barbecuing begins with the exclusive gas ignition system on this grill, which makes quick work of lighting charcoal briquets. All you do is push a button. A high-capacity ash catcher makes cleaning easy, too. The large charcoal storage container keeps charcoal dry.

This model also has the Dual-Purpose Thermometer, the Tuck-Away™ Lid Holder, and Char-Basket™ Fuel Holders.

## Weber®, Smokey Joe®, and Go-Anywhere® Grills

Smaller in size than the other Weber® grills, these transportable tabletop models cook the same way as their larger counterparts. They are available in charcoal and gas models.

## Weber® Genesis® 3000 Series Gas Barbecue

A convenient alternative to cooking with charcoal, this grill features specially angled Flavorizer® Bars that distribute the heat evenly and vaporize the drippings to create barbecue flavor without flare-ups. Stainless steel burners run the length of the cooking box, offering controlled, even cooking and energy efficiency.

This grill has 635 square inches (4,097 square cm) of cooking area and warming racks. Its durable porcelain-enameled cooking grate is easy to clean.

Other features include the Dual-Purpose Thermometer, weather-resistant wood work surfaces, and an easy-to-read fuel scale. Available in liquid propane and natural gas models.

# Grilling Techniques

### The Direct Method in a Charcoal Kettle

This grilling technique is best for relatively thin pieces of food that cook in less than 25 minutes; many steaks, chops and burgers fall in this category. Direct cooking is also used for boneless chicken breasts, fish fillets and steaks, and shellfish. The food is placed directly over the hot coals.

To prepare the grill, open all of the vents and spread charcoal briquets in a single solid layer that fills the charcoal grate. Next, mound the briquets in a pyramid-shaped pile and ignite them, keeping the lid off. When the briquets are lightly coated with gray ash (25 to 30 minutes), use long-handled tongs to spread them into a single layer again. Set the cooking grate in place and arrange the food on the grate. Place the lid on the grill, leaving all vents open, and grill as directed in your recipe, turning the food once halfway through the cooking time.

### The Direct Method in a Gas Barbecue

With gas grills, use of the Direct Method is limited to preheating and searing; most of the actual cooking is done by the Indirect Method.

To preheat the grill, open the lid and check that all burner control knobs are turned to OFF and the fuel scale reads more than "E." Turn on the gas at the source. Light with the igniter switch or, if necessary, a match (see the manufacturer's directions). Check through the viewing port to be sure the burner is lit. Close the lid, turn all burners to HIGH, and preheat 10 to 15 minutes to bring the grill to 500°–550°F (260°–288°C). Then adjust the heat controls as the recipe directs and proceed to cook the food. For searing techniques, see the box at right.

## Indirect Cooking in a Charcoal Kettle

Use this method for thick-cut pork chops and steaks that need to cook for more than 25 minutes at lower temperatures. This technique will also be used for roasts, ribs, whole fish, turkeys and chickens. The food is not turned, and the grill must be kept covered, since every time you open the lid, heat escapes and the cooking time increases.

To set up the grill for the Indirect Method, open all vents. Position Char-Basket™ Fuel Holders or charcoal rails on either side of the charcoal grate as close as possible to the outside edges. Divide the charcoal briquets evenly and place them in the holders (see the chart below for the number to use). Ignite the briquets and, keeping the lid off, let them burn until lightly covered with gray ash (25 to 30 minutes). If necessary, use long-handled tongs to rearrange briquets so the heat will be even.

Place a foil drip pan on the charcoal grate between the baskets of coals. Put the cooking grate in place, positioning the hinged sides of the grate over the briquets so that more can be added if necessary. Arrange the food in the center of the cooking grate. Place the lid on the grill, leaving all vents open, and grill as directed. If the food is to cook for more than an hour, add briquets as indicated on the chart.

## Indirect Cooking in a Gas Barbecue

Except when you are searing, the Indirect Method is always the best approach to cooking on a gas grill. Turn the food only if you are directed to do so in the recipe. The grill must be kept covered or you will have to increase the cooking time. Let foods grill for the minimum time specified in the recipe before checking for doneness.

When using the Indirect Method, preheat as directed for the Direct Method (facing page). Arrange the food in the center of the cooking grate and place the lid on the grill. For three-burner grills, set the front and back burners to MEDIUM and the center burner to OFF; for two-burner grills, turn the front and back burners to MEDIUM.

If you have another brand of grill, check your owner's manual for Indirect cooking instructions.

## Quick Smoke Flavoring

When you use a covered barbecue grill, wood chips or chunks placed beneath the cooking grate can add a delicate smoked flavor. Chips are ideal for foods with shorter cooking times; chunks are best for foods that take longer. The best woods for beef are hickory, oak, mesquite, and grapevine; for pork, choose alder, apple, cherry, grapevine, hickory, or mesquite; and for lamb, try apple, cherry, or oak. You may also want to experiment with orange peels, dried corn cobs, dried fennel stocks, garlic, or woody perennial fresh herbs.

Start by soaking the wood chips or chunks in water—30 minutes for chips, one hour for chunks.

In a charcoal grill, scatter a handful or two of the wet chips right over the hot coals. With a gas grill, turn the heat to HIGH and place the chips with a little bit of water in a small foil pan directly on the heat source in the left front corner of the grill. Used as directed, a Weber® Steam-N-Chips™ Smoker makes such quick smoking a snap. Preheat the barbecue as directed and cook by the Indirect Method on MEDIUM heat.

When the wood starts smoking, begin grilling, and keep the lid on. Add more soaked chips when you no longer see smoke exiting the vents. Remember, a little smoke goes a long way—you want the flavor to complement, not overpower, the food's natural taste.

### The Right Amount of Charcoal for Indirect Cooking

| Diameter of grill in inches | Briquets needed on each side for first hour | Number of briquets to add to each side every hour |
|---|---|---|
| 26 ¾" (68 cm) | 30 | 9 |
| 22 ½" (57 cm) | 25 | 8 |
| 18 ½" (47 cm) | 16 | 5 |

# Fuels & Fire Starters

**Charcoal briquets.** Long the outdoor chef's favorite fuel, charcoal briquets are manufactured from pulverized charcoal and additives that make them easy to light. Once ignited, briquets provide good even heat, but the various brands differ somewhat in composition and density. Top-quality brands burn longer and more evenly. Store briquets in a dry place.

**Self-starting briquets.** Impregnated with a liquid starter, these briquets ignite with a match and heat up quickly. *Do not add self-starting briquets to an existing hot fire*—the fuel in them burns off slowly and it can spoil the flavor of the food. Always use regular briquets when additional charcoal is needed.

**Liquid starter.** If you use a liquid starter, be sure it's a product intended for charcoal, and follow the manufacturer's instructions closely. Let the starter soak into the coals for a few minutes; then ignite in several places. *Never* pour liquid starter on hot coals—this can cause a dangerous flare-up.

**Solid starter.** Solid starters such as Weber® FireStarters are safe, nontoxic, odorless cubes that light easily with a match and burn without further attention. Mound the briquets in a pyramid shape on top of the cubes, leaving a corner of the cubes exposed. Ignite the cubes, and the coals will be ready in 25 to 30 minutes.

**Chimney starter.** The metal cannister on this device holds a supply of charcoal briquets a few inches above the charcoal grate. Light two Weber® FireStarters or some wadded newspapers underneath the chimney, and it will bring the coals quickly to readiness.

**Electric starter.** Comprised of a large heating element, a handle, and an electrical cord, this device nestles in a bed of unlit briquets and ignites them when the cord is connected. After 10 minutes, remove the starter (if you leave it in too long, the heating element will burn out).

**Liquid propane and natural gas.** Gas barbecues use either liquid propane or natural gas as fuel. Liquid propane is stored in a refillable tank mounted on the barbecue grill. Expect 20 to 30 hours of use from a tank. Natural gas is piped to a grill through a permanent hookup to a gas line. *Note:* Never use one kind of fuel in a barbecue grill designed for the other.

*Follow the manufacturer's instructions carefully and heed the rules below to ensure safety while you grill.*

- *Never leave a hot grill unattended. Keep children and pets at a safe distance.*

- *Never use a charcoal or gas grill indoors or in a closed garage or enclosed patio.*

- *Do not use gasoline or other highly volatile fluids as charcoal lighters.*

- *Do not add liquid starter to hot—or even warm—coals.*

- *Place your grill in an open, level area away from the house, wood railings, trees, bushes, or other combustible surfaces.*

- *Do not attempt to barbecue in high winds.*

- *Wear an insulated, fire-retardant barbecue mitt and use long-handled tools designed for grilling. Do not wear clothing with loose, flowing sleeves.*

# Buying & Storing Meat

## How Much to Buy

From a strictly nutritional standpoint, the recommended serving of lean, boneless cooked meat is 3 ounces (85 g); about 4 ounces (115 g) of uncooked meat will yield that size serving. Many people enjoy eating more than that, however.

When you're buying beefsteak, remember that cuts with more bone and fat will give you fewer servings per pound. Count on 1 or 2 servings per pound of T-bone steak; 2 or 3 servings per pound of porterhouse, sirloin, rib, or rib-eye steak; and 3 or 4 servings per pound of tenderloin or top loin steak.

## Storage Tips

Uncooked meat should be kept in the refrigerator for short-term storage; the length of time the meat will remain fresh depends on the type of meat, its freshness when purchased, and the storage temperature. To keep prepackaged meat in the refrigerator for more than 2 days, discard the original package and store the meat loosely wrapped (but not so loosely that it dries out).

For longer storage, freeze the meat after wrapping it airtight in moistureproof freezer wrap. Place a double thickness of wax paper between steaks, chops, and ground meat patties so they won't stick together. Label the packages with the cut of meat, the weight or number of servings, and the date. Freeze at 0°F (-18°C).

It's always best to thaw meat, well wrapped, in the refrigerator, rather than at room temperature. You can refreeze meat that has been partially thawed in the refrigerator, but expect some loss of quality.

## Refrigerator & Freezer Storage Times for Meats

| Cut of meat | Refrigerator storage at 36°–40°F (2°–4°C) | Freezer storage at 0°F (–18°C) |
|---|---|---|
| Ground meats | 1–2 days | 3 months |
| Chops | 3–5 days | 4 months |
| Pork & veal steaks | 3–5 days | 4–6 months |
| Beef & lamb steaks | 3–5 days | 6–12 months |

## Alternative Names for Some Popular Beefsteaks

| Cut of Meat | Alternate Names |
|---|---|
| Rib eye steak, boneless | Delmonico steak, Spencer |
| Rib steak | Spencer |
| Shell sirloin steak, bone-in | New York sirloin |
| Tenderloin steak | filet mignon, beef fillet, beef medallion |
| Top loin steak | shell, strip, club, club sirloin, sirloin strip, Kansas City, New York strip |
| Top round steak | London broil, top round center cut |

# Grilling Guide for Steaks, Chops & Burgers

| Cut of Meat | Thickness or Weight | Approximate Cooking Time |
|---|---|---|
| **BEEF** | | |
| Place steaks on cooking grate, using Direct Method for a charcoal grill, Indirect Method/Medium Heat for a gas grill. Cook for the time listed in this chart, based on medium-rare (145°F/63°C), or until desired doneness; turn once halfway through the cooking time. Sear, if desired. | | |
| Steaks (T-bone, New York, | 1 inch (2.5 cm) | 10–12 minutes |
|     porterhouse, tenderloin, top | 1½ inches (3.5 cm) | 14–16 minutes |
|     round, sirloin, rib-eye, fillet) | 2 inches (5 cm) | 20–25 minutes |
| Flank steak | 1–2 lbs (455–905 g) | 12–15 minutes |
| Skirt steak | ¼–½ inch (6 mm–1 cm) | 7–9 minutes |
| **VEAL & LAMB** | | |
| Place chops on cooking grate, using Direct Method for a charcoal grill, Indirect Method/Medium Heat for a gas grill. Cook for time given in chart, based on medium (160°F/71°C) for veal and medium-rare (145°F/63°C) for lamb, or until desired doneness; turn once halfway through cooking time. Sear, if desired. | | |
| Veal chops (rib, loin) | ¾ inch (2 cm) | 10–12 minutes |
| | 1 inch (2.5 cm) | 12–14 minutes |
| | 1½ inches (3.5 cm) | 16–18 minutes |
| Lamb chops (rib, loin, shoulder) | 1 inch (2.5 cm) | 10 minutes |
| | 1½ inches (3.5 cm) | 12–14 minutes |
| **PORK** | | |
| Place chops on cooking grate. On a charcoal grill, use Direct Method for 3/4- to 1-inch (2- to 2.5-cm) thickness, and the Indirect Method for thicker chops. On a gas grill use Indirect Method/Medium Heat for all chops. Cook for time given in chart, based on medium (160°F/71°C), or until meat near bone is no longer pink; turn once halfway through cooking time. Sear, if desired. | | |
| Chops (rib, loin, shoulder) | ¾ inch (2 cm) | 10–12 minutes |
| | 1 inch (2.5 cm) | 12–14 minutes |
| | 1¼–1½ inches (3–3.5 cm) | 25–35 minutes |
| **BURGERS** | | |
| Place patties on cooking grate, using Direct Method for a charcoal grill, Indirect Method/Medium Heat for a gas grill. Cook for time given in chart or until no longer pink in center and juices run clear; turn once halfway through cooking time. | | |
| Lean ground beef, lamb, pork | ¾ inch (2 cm) | 160°F (71°C) for medium; about 10 minutes |
| Lean ground chicken, turkey | ¾ inch (2 cm) | 165°F (74°C) for medium-well; 10–12 minutes |

# MARINADES & BASTES FOR MEAT

Flavorful marinades and bastes offer a variety of ways to enhance and enliven the naturally rich tastes of grilled meats. A marinade containing wine, vinegar, or citrus juice is the best choice for less tender cuts—the acidic liquid helps tenderize the meat. Tender cuts of meat benefit from a baste applied while the meat grills.

## Wine & Garlic Marinade for Beef or Lamb

1   cup (240 ml) dry red wine

2   tablespoons *each* red wine vinegar and olive oil

2   cloves garlic, minced or pressed

1   tablespoon minced fresh rosemary or 1 teaspoon crumbled dried rosemary

In a small bowl, combine wine, vinegar, oil, garlic, and rosemary. Marinate beef or lamb in wine mixture for at least 4 hours or until next day.

MAKES ABOUT 1¼ CUPS (300 ML), ENOUGH FOR 4 TO 6 SERVINGS OF MEAT.

*Per serving:* 85 calories (88% from fat), 5 g total fat (1 g saturated fat), 0 mg cholesterol, 3 mg sodium, 2 g carbohydrates, 0 g fiber, 0 g protein, 9 mg calcium, 0 mg iron

## Parsley-Orange Baste for Lamb or Pork

½   cup (120 ml) balsamic vinegar

¼   cup (60 ml) minced parsley

2   tablespoons *each* lemon juice and honey

1   tablespoon grated orange peel

In a small bowl, combine vinegar, parsley, lemon juice, honey, and orange peel. Brush parsley-orange mixture all over lamb or pork while it cooks.

MAKES ABOUT 1 CUP (240 ML), ENOUGH FOR 4 TO 6 SERVINGS OF MEAT.

*Per serving:* 32 calories (0% from fat), 0 g total fat (0 g saturated fat), 0 mg cholesterol, 4 mg sodium, 9 g carbohydrates, 0 g fiber, 0 g protein, 7 mg calcium, 0 mg iron

## Lemon-Dijon Marinade for Veal or Beef

¼   cup (60 ml) olive oil or salad oil

¼   cup (60 ml) *each* white wine vinegar, minced shallots, and Dijon mustard

2   cloves garlic, minced or pressed

1   tablespoon lemon juice

1   teaspoon grated lemon peel

In a small bowl, combine oil, vinegar, shallots, mustard, garlic, lemon juice, and lemon peel. Marinate veal or beef in the lemon-Dijon mixture for at least 4 hours or until next day.

MAKES ABOUT 1 CUP (240 ML), ENOUGH FOR ABOUT 4 SERVINGS OF MEAT.

*Per serving:* 147 calories (90% from fat), 14 g total fat (2 g saturated fat), 0 mg cholesterol, 362 mg sodium, 3 g carbohydrates, 0 g fiber, 0 g protein, 8 mg calcium, 0 mg iron

# Glossary

**BASTE**
Seasoned liquid brushed over food as it cooks to keep surface moist and add flavor

**BUTTERFLY**
To make a horizontal cut through middle of a thick piece of meat, leaving about 1 inch (2.5 cm) uncut, and then opening piece out and flattening it

**CARVING BOARD**
Wooden board with a well for catching juices from meat as it is being carved

**CHARCOAL BRIQUETS**
Compact 2-inch (5-cm) pieces of fuel made of charcoal and additives; when ignited, they provide even heat for cooking

**CHAR-BASKET™ FUEL HOLDERS**
Hold charcoal against sides of grill to provide a larger cooking area when Indirect Method is used; charcoal rails serve the same function

**COOKING GRATE**
Metal grill on which food is cooked; hinged sides facilitate addition of charcoal briquets

**DEGLAZE**
To loosen drippings on bottom of a roasting or frying pan by stirring in wine, stock, or another liquid

**DIRECT METHOD**
Grilling technique, used for small or thin cuts of meat and other foods that cook in less than 25 minutes; the food is cooked directly over heat source and turned once halfway through grilling time; on a gas grill, used only for preheating and searing

**DRY RUB**
Highly concentrated blend of herbs and spices that is rubbed all over food before cooking to impart flavor

**DRIP PAN**
Foil pan placed beneath food to catch melted fat and juices when food is cooked by Indirect Method

**GLAZE**
To coat with a baste or sauce, so as to give a sheen to cooked food

**GRIDDLE**
Heavy, flat pan with a metal handle usually made of cast iron and used to cook breakfast fare, fajitas, or grilled sandwiches

**GRILL BRUSH**
Stiff brass bristle brush used for removing stubborn food residue from the cooking grate

**GRILLING**
Cooking food on a metal grate over a heat source (charcoal, gas, or electric coil)

**INDIRECT METHOD**
Grilling technique, used primarily for larger cuts of meat and other foods that require cooking times longer than 25 minutes; food is cooked by reflected heat (not directly above heat source), sealing in juices and eliminating the need for turning; this method can only be used with a covered grill

**INSTANT-READ THERMOMETER**
Type of meat thermometer that registers the internal temperature of food within seconds of being inserted; they are not safe for use in the oven

**MARINADE**
Seasoned liquid (usually containing an acidic ingredient, such as vinegar, wine, or citrus juice) in which food soaks, tenderizing it and enhancing flavor

**SEAR**
To brown meat directly above heat source at a high temperature, for just a brief time, to seal in juices

**SKEWER**
Thin metal or bamboo sticks of various lengths on which pieces of meat, poultry, fish, or vegetables are secured prior to grilling

**SPATULA**
Flat, thin tool used to turn and lift foods on the grill

**TONGS**
Tool used to grasp and turn foods; usually made of metal with two pieces joined at one end

**WOOD CHIPS**
Small chips of dried, fragrant hardwoods used to impart a smoky flavor to foods

**WOOD CHUNKS**
Chunks of dried, fragrant hardwoods used either as a fuel or to add smoky flavor to foods as they cook

**ZEST**
Thin, outermost layer of peel (colored part only) of citrus fruits

# Grilled Steak

*Sirloin, porterhouse, club, rib, and fillet are all well-suited for these recipes. Cheese lovers will leap tall buildings for the blue-cheese variation described below.*

| Charcoal | Direct |
|---|---|
| Gas | Indirect/Medium Heat Searing (optional) see page 6 |
| Grilling time | 10–12 minutes |

4   beefsteaks, 8 to 10 ounces (230 to 285 g) *each,* cut about 1 inch (2.5 cm) thick, trimmed of fat

Salt and pepper

Very Easy

*Blue Cheese Steak*

### Basic Steak
Arrange steaks on cooking grate. Place lid on grill. Cook, turning once halfway through cooking time, until meat is done to your liking (10 to 12 minutes for medium-rare; cut to test). Season to taste with salt and pepper.

MAKES 4 SERVINGS.

*Per serving:* 242 calories (45% from fat), 12 g total fat (5 g saturated fat), 90 mg cholesterol, 75 mg sodium, 0 g carbohydrates, 0 g fiber, 32 g protein, 8 mg calcium, 3 mg iron

4   ounces (115g) crumbled blue-veined cheese

¼   cup (60 ml) thinly sliced green onions

Basic Steak (see above)

### Blue Cheese Steak
Combine cheese and onions in a small bowl. Follow directions for Basic Steak, sprinkling meat with cheese mixture after steaks are turned.

*Per serving:* 363 calories (54% from fat), 21 g total fat (11 g saturated fat), 116 mg cholesterol, 547 mg sodium, 1 g carbohydrates, 0 g fiber, 39 g protein, 191 mg calcium, 4 mg iron

1½   teaspoons dried basil

1   teaspoon *each* dried tarragon and dried chives

4   cloves garlic, minced or pressed

Basic Steak (see above)

### Savory Herbed Steak
Combine basil, tarragon, chives, and garlic in a small bowl. Follow directions for Basic Steak, patting herb mixture all over steaks, pressing into surface, before grilling. Omit salt and pepper.

*Per serving:* 250 calories (44% from fat), 12 g total fat (5 g saturated fat), 90 mg cholesterol, 76 mg sodium, 2 g carbohydrates, 0 g fiber, 32 g protein, 35 mg calcium, 4 mg iron

# Tequila Beefsteaks

*A splash of tequila in the marinade gives New York strip steaks a tantalizing flavor.*

| | |
|---|---|
| **Charcoal** | Direct |
| **Gas** | Indirect/Medium Heat Searing (optional) see page 6 |
| **Marinating time** | 1 hour or until next day |
| **Grilling time** | 12–14 minutes |

½ cup (120 ml) tequila

2 tablespoons olive oil

1 tablespoon pepper

2 teaspoons grated lemon zest

1 large clove garlic, minced or pressed

4 New York strip steaks, 8 to 10 ounces (230 to 285 g) *each,* cut 1 to 1½ inches (2.5 to 3.5 cm) thick, trimmed of fat

Salt

**Very Easy**

Combine tequila, oil, pepper, lemon zest, and garlic in a large heavy-duty plastic food bag or nonreactive bowl. Add steaks and seal bag (or cover bowl). Rotate bag to distribute marinade and place in a shallow pan. Refrigerate for 1 hour or until the next day, turning meat occasionally.

Remove steaks and drain, reserving marinade. Arrange steaks on cooking grate. Place lid on grill. Cook, turning and brushing once with reserved marinade halfway through cooking time, until meat is done to your liking (12 to 14 minutes for medium-rare; cut to test). Season to taste with salt.

MAKES 4 SERVINGS.

*Per serving:* 359 calories (46% from fat), 18 g total fat (5 g saturated fat), 134 mg cholesterol, 100 mg sodium, 2 g carbohydrates, 0 g fiber, 46 g protein, 27 mg calcium, 6 mg iron

# Steak with Tomato Relish

*This recipe makes full use of the grill since the robust tomato relish that makes the dish special is prepared right alongside the meat.*

| | |
|---|---|
| Charcoal | Direct |
| Gas | Indirect/Medium Heat<br>Searing (optional) see page 6 |
| Grilling time | 20–25 minutes |

1   bone-in steak, 2½ to 3 pounds (1.15 to 1.35 kg), such as T-bone or porterhouse, or 1 boneless steak, 1½ to 2 pounds (680 to 905 g), such as top round or sirloin, about 2 inches (5 cm) thick, trimmed of fat

8   medium-size pear-shaped (Roma-type) tomatoes, halved lengthwise

2   tablespoons olive oil

1   large onion, chopped

1   clove garlic, minced or pressed

½   cup (120 ml) chopped fresh basil or ¼ cup (60 ml) dried basil

    Salt and pepper

Arrange steak on cooking grate. Arrange tomatoes, cut side up, around steak and brush tops lightly with some of the oil. Place lid on grill. Cook, turning tomatoes once when browned on bottom, until tomatoes are soft when pressed (7 to 10 minutes). Meanwhile, combine remaining oil, onion, and garlic in an 8- to 10-inch (20- to 25-cm) metal-handled frying pan.

Remove tomatoes from grill and set aside. Set frying pan on grate, turn meat over, and place lid on grill. Cook, stirring onion mixture occasionally, until onion is tinged with gold (8 to 10 minutes) and meat is done to your liking (20 to 25 minutes total for medium-rare; cut to test).

Stir basil and tomatoes into onion mixture. Place meat on a board with a well or on a platter. Cut meat away from bone, if present; slicing thinly across the grain. If you wish, spoon accumulated meat juices into tomato relish. Season to taste with salt and pepper. Serve with relish.

MAKES 4 TO 6 SERVINGS.

*Per serving:* 351 calories (45% from fat), 18 g total fat (5 g saturated fat), 89 mg cholesterol, 89 mg sodium, 15 g carbohydrates, 3 g fiber, 34 g protein, 106 mg calcium, 6 mg iron

# Rib-eye Steak with Tapenade

*Tapenade, a highly flavorful olive spread, is rubbed all over a butterflied beef roast that has been braced with skewers to make the grilling easy.*

| Charcoal | Direct |
|---|---|
| Gas | Indirect/Medium Heat<br>Searing (optional) see page 6 |
| Grilling time | 20–25 minutes |

| | |
|---|---|
| 1¼ | cups (300 ml) calamata (brine-cured) or oil-cured olives |
| 2 | cloves garlic |
| 1½ | teaspoons freshly ground pepper |
| ¾ | teaspoon grated lemon zest |
| 1 | tablespoon lemon juice |
| 2 | canned anchovy fillets, drained |
| 1 | boned rib-eye beef roast, 2½ to 3¾ pounds (1.15 to 1.7 kg), 4 to 6 inches (10 to 15 cm) long, trimmed of fat |

Good for a Crowd

Pinch or cut pits from olives. Place olives in a food processor with garlic, pepper, lemon zest, lemon juice, and anchovies. Blend until coarsely puréed. If made ahead, cover tapenade and refrigerate for up to 1 week.

Make a horizontal cut through middle of meat, leaving about 1 inch (2.5 cm) uncut, and lay meat open. With your palms, press meat to flatten evenly. Thread 2 long metal skewers lengthwise through beef, placing skewers parallel to each other and about 3 inches (8 cm) apart. Rub meat all over with 2 or 3 tablespoons of the tapenade.

Arrange steak on cooking grate. Place lid on grill. Cook, turning once halfway through cooking time, until meat is done to your liking (20 to 25 minutes for medium-rare; cut to test). Slice meat thinly across grain. Serve with remaining tapenade.

MAKES 8 TO 12 SERVINGS.

*Per serving:* 246 calories (55% from fat), 15 g total fat (5 g saturated fat), 68 mg cholesterol, 395 mg sodium, 3 g carbohydrates, 0 g fiber, 24 g protein, 16 mg calcium, 2 mg iron

# Steak, Potato & Onion Grill

*A tangy mustard butter coats tender wedges of potatoes, which are grilled alongside a thick steak. More of the same butter mixture is then warmed on the grill to serve as a sauce with the meal.*

| Charcoal | Direct |
|---|---|
| Gas | Indirect/Medium Heat<br>Searing (optional) see page 6 |
| Grilling time | 25–30 minutes |

18   green onions

2   quarts (1.9 liters) cold water mixed with 2 teaspoons salt

6   medium-size white thin-skinned potatoes, scrubbed

½   cup (120 ml) butter or margarine, melted

3   tablespoons Dijon mustard

¼   cup (60 ml) minced shallots

1   bone-in steak, 2½ to 3 pounds (1.15 to 1.35 kg), such as T-bone or porterhouse, or 1 boneless steak, 1½ to 2 pounds (680 to 905 g), such as sirloin or top round, cut about 2 inches (5 cm) thick, trimmed of fat

Peel off outer layer from onions and trim tops, leaving about 4 inches (10 cm) of green. Immerse in salted water. Cut potatoes lengthwise into eighths and immerse with onions. Let stand for 5 minutes. Meanwhile, combine butter, mustard, and shallots in a 1- to 1½-quart (950-ml to 1.4-liter) metal-handled pan.

Remove potatoes from water and drain. Mix with half the mustard butter and set aside.

Arrange steak on cooking grate. Place lid on grill. Cook for 5 minutes. Arrange potatoes on grate without overlapping. Cook, turning meat and potatoes once halfway through cooking time, until potatoes are tender when pierced (about 15 minutes) and meat is done to your liking (20 to 25 minutes total for medium-rare; cut to test). Transfer to a platter and keep warm.

Remove onions from water and drain. Arrange on grate. Set pan with remaining mustard butter on grate. Place lid on grill. Cook, turning onions once, until sauce is hot and onions are lightly browned (about 5 minutes).

Cut meat away from bone, if present; slice thinly across grain. Arrange onions alongside meat. Serve with remaining mustard butter.

MAKES 4 TO 6 SERVINGS.

*Per serving:* 645 calories (48% from fat), 34 g total fat (18 g saturated fat), 162 g cholesterol, 737 mg sodium, 38 g carbohydrates, 4 g fiber, 44 g protein, 56 mg calcium, 6 mg iron

**GRILL BY THE BOOK**
**T I P**

Tongs are best for turning meats; a fork will pierce the flesh and allow juices to escape.

# GREAT GRILLED POTATOES & ONIONS

Potatoes and onions are natural partners for many grilled meats. They are also convenient side dishes to prepare, since they can often be grilled right alongside the meat. Onions cook to toasty perfection on the grill and seem to taste sweeter and chewier when prepared in this manner. And few things are more pleasing to a true steak lover than a generous side order of crisply grilled, golden brown potatoes.

## Grilled Balsamic Potatoes

| Charcoal | Direct |
|---|---|
| Gas | Indirect/Medium Heat |
| Grilling time | 25–30 minutes |

2   pounds (905 g) small red thin-skinned potatoes, about 1½ inches (3.5 cm) in diameter, scrubbed and cut in half crosswise

3   tablespoons olive oil

3   tablespoons balsamic vinegar

½   cup (120 ml) thinly sliced green onions

¼   cup (60 ml) finely chopped parsley

Salt and freshly ground pepper

Lightly brush potatoes all over with oil. Arrange potatoes, cut side down, on cooking grate. Place lid on grill. Cook, turning once halfway through cooking time, until potatoes are browned and tender when pierced (25 to 30 minutes).

In a large bowl, gently mix potatoes with vinegar and remaining oil. Stir in onions and parsley. Season to taste with salt and pepper.

MAKES 6 TO 8 SERVINGS.

*Per serving:* 160 calories (34% calories from fat), 6 g total fat (1 g saturated fat), 0 mg cholesterol, 12 mg sodium, 24 g carbohydrates, 2 g fiber, 3 g protein, 8 mg calcium, 1 mg iron

**Very Easy**

## Roasted Red Onions & Tomatoes

| Charcoal | Direct |
|---|---|
| Gas | Indirect/Medium Heat |
| Grilling time | About 1 hour |

2   medium-size red onions, cut lengthwise into slivers

2   tablespoons olive oil

Salt and pepper

8   medium-size tomatoes, cut in half horizontally

1   tablespoon minced garlic

In a 9- by 13-inch (23- by 33-cm) foil pan, combine onions and 1 tablespoon of the oil; sprinkle with salt and pepper. Stir to coat onions well. Place tomatoes, cut side up, over onion mixture. Brush tomatoes with remaining oil; sprinkle with more salt and pepper. Pat garlic on tomatoes.

Set pan on cooking grate. Place lid on grill. Cook until juices have evaporated and onions begin to caramelize (about 1 hour). Check tomatoes after 30 minutes; if cooking is uneven, use a spatula to move tomatoes and onions around in pan.

MAKES 8 SERVINGS.

*Per serving:* 80 calories (40% calories from fat), 4 g total fat (8 g saturated fat), 0 mg cholesterol, 18 mg sodium, 11 g carbohydrates, 3 g fiber, 2 g protein, 21 mg calcium, 1 mg iron

## Herbed Roasted Onions

| Charcoal | Direct |
|---|---|
| Gas | Indirect/Medium Heat |
| Grilling time | 50–60 minutes |

⅓ cup (80 ml) balsamic vinegar

4 teaspoons sugar

½ cup (120 ml) chicken broth

6 onions, 2½ to 3 inches (6 to 8 cm) in diameter, unpeeled, cut in half vertically

1 tablespoon chopped fresh thyme or 1 teaspoon dried thyme

Thyme sprigs (optional)

Salt

In a 9- by 13-inch (23- by 33-cm) foil pan, combine vinegar, sugar, and ¼ cup (60 ml) of the broth. Place onions, cut side down, in pan. Sprinkle with chopped thyme.

Set pan on cooking grate. Place lid on grill. Cook until most of the liquid has evaporated (40 to 45 minutes). Add remaining broth and gently stir to loosen browned drippings at edges. Continue to cook until onions are tender when pressed (10 to 15 more minutes).

Remove pan from grill; if pan is dry, add 2 to 3 tablespoons water, tilting pan to moisten bottom. Let onions stand for about 10 minutes. Transfer onions to a serving bowl. Garnish with thyme sprigs, if desired. Season to taste with salt. Serve warm or at room temperature.

MAKES 6 SERVINGS.

*Per serving:* 80 calories (5% calories from fat), 0 g total fat (0 g saturated fat), 0 mg cholesterol, 89 mg sodium, 18 g carbohydrates, 3 g fiber, 2 g protein, 39 mg calcium, 1 mg iron

## New Potatoes & Garlic Grilled in Foil

| Charcoal | Direct |
|---|---|
| Gas | Indirect/Medium Heat |
| Grilling time | About 30 minutes |

24 small new potatoes, scrubbed and cut in half

24 to 30 large cloves garlic

½ cup (120 ml) minced shallots

6 small fresh rosemary sprigs

6 teaspoons *each* olive oil and lemon juice

Salt and pepper

On each of 6 pieces of heavy-duty foil about 10 by 16 inches (25 by 40 cm), lay potatoes, garlic, shallots, and rosemary, dividing equally. Evenly sprinkle with oil and lemon juice. Season to taste with salt and pepper. Bring foil edges up over food and crimp well to seal.

Arrange foil bundles on cooking grate. Place lid on grill. Cook until potatoes are tender when pierced (about 30 minutes). Transfer bundles to individual plates. To open, slash a cross through foil in top of each bundle; discard rosemary.

MAKES 6 SERVINGS.

*Per serving:* 201 calories (22% calories from fat), 5 g total fat (1 g saturated fat), 0 mg cholesterol, 18 mg sodium, 36 g carbohydrates, 3 g fiber, 4 g protein, 45 mg calcium, 2 mg iron

# Stuffed London Broil & New Potatoes

*This steak has a stuffing of gremolata, a flavorful mixture of minced parsley, garlic, and grated lemon zest. Accompanying the meat to the grill are precooked potatoes, bathed in a tangy vinegar-based sauce.*

| | |
|---|---|
| **Charcoal** | Direct |
| **Gas** | Indirect/Medium Heat Searing (optional) see page 6 |
| **Grilling time** | 20–25 minutes |

1 piece, 2½ to 2¾ pounds (1.15 to 1.25 kg), first-cut top round beef (sometimes called London broil), cut about 2 inches (5 cm) thick, trimmed of fat

¼ cup (60 ml) minced parsley

3 cloves garlic, minced or pressed

2 tablespoons grated lemon zest

About ½ cup (120 ml) mesquite, apple, or hickory wood chips

3 to 3½ pounds (1.35 to 1.6 kg) small red thin-skinned potatoes, scrubbed

½ cup (120 ml) balsamic or red wine vinegar

3 tablespoons Dijon mustard

1 tablespoon olive oil

Lowfat

With a long, sharp knife, cut a horizontal pocket about three-quarters of the way through meat on a long side. Combine parsley, garlic, and lemon zest; spread evenly inside pocket. Wrap airtight and refrigerate for up to 6 hours.

Place wood chips in a bowl. Add enough warm water to make them float; soak 30 minutes. Add potatoes to 3 quarts (2.8 liters) water in a 5- to 6-quart (5- to 6-liter) pan. Bring to a boil over high heat; reduce heat, cover, and simmer the potatoes until barely tender when pierced (15 to 20 minutes). Drain; return to pan.

Combine vinegar, mustard, and oil in a small bowl. Add half the vinegar mixture to potatoes; mix well. Thread potatoes on long metal skewers. Push a second skewer through potatoes, parallel to first. Set aside.

*In a charcoal barbecue,* drain wood chips and scatter on the mounds of coals. *In a gas barbecue,* place chips in a foil pan and set under cooking grate on top of heat source in left front corner of barbecue; turn heat to high and preheat for 10 to 15 minutes. Arrange meat on cooking grate. Place lid on grill. (*In a gas barbecue,* turn heat to Indirect/Medium.) Cook for 5 minutes. Add skewers. Cook, turning meat and potatoes once halfway through cooking time and brushing potatoes with remaining vinegar mixture, until potatoes are tender when pierced (18 to 20 minutes) and meat is done to your liking (20 to 25 minutes total for medium-rare; cut to test). Slice meat across grain and arrange on a platter with potatoes.

MAKES 6 TO 8 SERVINGS.

*Per serving:* 430 calories (18% from fat), 9 g total fat (2 g saturated fat), 107 mg cholesterol, 250 mg sodium, 39 g carbohydrates, 4 g fiber, 45 g protein, 15 mg calcium, 5 mg iron

# Olive-stuffed Steak

*Green olives with pimentos dot slices of this butterflied rump roast. The secret ingredients in the marinade are garlic salad dressing mix and liquid drained from the olives.*

| | |
|---|---|
| **Charcoal** | Indirect<br>Searing (optional) see page 6 |
| **Gas** | Indirect/Medium Heat<br>Searing (optional) see page 6 |
| **Marinating time** | 6 hours or until next day |
| **Grilling time** | 12–14 minutes |

1   boneless beef rump roast or chuck roast, about 4 pounds (1.8 kg), trimmed of fat

1   jar, about 3 ounces (85 g), pimento-stuffed green olives

¼   cup (60 ml) *each* wine vinegar and olive oil

1   package, 0.75 ounce (22 g), garlic salad dressing mix

1   tablespoon dehydrated onion flakes

1   teaspoon lemon pepper

Good for a Crowd

If using a rump roast, make a lengthwise horizontal cut through middle of meat, leaving about 1 inch (2.5 cm) uncut, and lay meat open. With your palms, press meat to flatten evenly; you should have a long steak about 2 inches (5 cm) thick. If using chuck roast, butterflying is not necessary.

Drain olives, reserving juice. Make cuts about 1 inch (2.5 cm) deep in meat; push an olive into each cut. Combine reserved olive juice, vinegar, oil, dressing mix, onion, and lemon pepper in a large heavy-duty plastic food bag. Add steak and seal bag securely. Rotate bag to distribute marinade and place in a shallow pan. Refrigerate for at least 6 hours or until the next day, turning bag occasionally.

Remove steak and drain, reserving marinade. Arrange meat in center of cooking grate. Place lid on grill. Cook, brushing occasionally with reserved marinade, until meat is done to your liking (30 to 35 minutes for medium-rare; cut to test). Slice meat thinly across grain.

MAKES 10 SERVINGS.

*Per serving:* 387 calories (61% from fat), 25 g total fat (8 g saturated fat), 108 mg cholesterol, 409 mg sodium, 1 g carbohydrates, 0 g fiber, 36 g protein, 9 mg calcium, 4 mg iron

# Beef Tenderloin & Vegetable Salad

*Grill the beef and vegetables up to a day ahead and serve them chilled on a bed of peppery arugula, accompanied with a tangy mayonnaise made with sun-dried tomatoes.*

| Charcoal | Indirect |
|---|---|
| Gas | Indirect/Medium Heat Searing (optional) see page 6 |
| Grilling time | 25–35 minutes |

Dried Tomato Mayonnaise (see below)

| | |
|---|---|
| 3 | tablespoons extra-virgin olive oil |
| ¼ | cup (60 ml) balsamic or red wine vinegar |
| 1½ | pounds (680 g) beef tenderloin, trimmed of fat |
| | Salt and freshly ground pepper |
| 4 | *each* small Oriental eggplants and zucchini, cut in half lengthwise |
| 4 | small red onions, peeled and cut in half crosswise |
| 4 | cups (950 ml) arugula or other salad greens, rinsed and crisped |
| 2 | ounces (55 g) thinly shaved Parmesan cheese |

## Dried Tomato Mayonnaise

| | |
|---|---|
| ¼ | cup (60 ml) drained and minced sun-dried tomatoes in olive oil |
| ¾ | cup (180 ml) mayonnaise |
| 2 | teaspoons balsamic or red wine vinegar |

Combine ingredients for Dried Tomato Mayonnaise in a small bowl. Cover and refrigerate until ready to use or for up to 2 days.

Combine 2 tablespoons of the oil and 3 tablespoons of the vinegar in a small bowl; set aside.

Lightly sprinkle meat with salt and pepper. Arrange beef in center of cooking grate. Place lid on grill. Cook for 15 minutes. Add eggplants, zucchini, and onions; brush with some of the vinegar mixture. Cook, turning vegetables once halfway through cooking time, until vegetables are soft when pressed (10 to 12 minutes for eggplants; about 15 minutes for zucchini and onions) and an instant-read thermometer inserted in thickest part of meat registers 145°F (63°C) for medium-rare (25 to 35 minutes total). Remove vegetables and meat from grill and let cool. If made ahead, wrap separately and refrigerate until the next day. Bring to room temperature before using.

Slice meat thinly across grain. Mix arugula with remaining oil and vinegar. Mound on 4 dinner plates and sprinkle with cheese. Add meat, eggplant, zucchini, and onions. Serve with Dried Tomato Mayonnaise and salt and pepper.

MAKES 4 SERVINGS.

*Per serving:* 889 calories (68% from fat), 68 g total fat (15 g saturated fat), 139 mg cholesterol, 594 mg sodium, 26 g carbohydrates, 5 g fiber, 46 g protein, 302 mg calcium, 7mg iron

**GRILL BY THE BOOK**
**T I P**

Arugula, also called rocket or roquette, is a tender, peppery green. Some varieties have smooth-edged leaves; others have serrated leaves.

# Steak, Fennel & Arugula Salad

*Grilled steak, spicy arugula, tangy green olives, and a hint of licorice from crisp, sliced fennel lend a cascade of flavors and textures to this salad.*

| Charcoal | Direct |
| --- | --- |
| Gas | Indirect/Medium Heat Searing (optional) see page 6 |
| Grilling time | 3–5 minutes |

1   large bulb fennel

1   New York (top loin) steak, about 1 pound (455 g), trimmed of fat

6   tablespoons garlic, onion, or herb vinegar

3   tablespoons extra-virgin olive oil

1   tablespoon minced fresh garlic

6   cups (1.4 liters) arugula or other salad greens, rinsed and crisped

1   cup (240 ml) pitted green olives

    Salt and pepper

Trim root end of fennel; cut off and discard leaves and stems. Halve bulb vertically. Slice crosswise into thin strips; set aside.

Cut steak across grain into strips about ¼ inch (6 mm) thick. In a bowl, mix meat with 3 tablespoons of the vinegar, 1 teaspoon of the oil, and garlic. In another bowl, combine remaining vinegar and oil; set aside. Place arugula and fennel in a shallow serving dish; set aside.

Arrange meat on cooking grate. Place lid on grill. Cook, turning once halfway through cooking time, until meat is done to your liking (3 to 5 minutes for medium-rare; cut to test). Arrange meat and olives over greens. Drizzle with vinegar mixture and season to taste with salt and pepper. Toss gently.

MAKES 4 SERVINGS.

*Per serving:* 337 calories (60% from fat), 23 g total fat (5 g saturated fat), 65 g cholesterol, 1004 mg sodium, 7 g carbohydrates, 3 g fiber, 27 g protein, 139 mg calcium, 4 mg iron

# Mexican Tri-tip with Rice & Beans

*To give this roast an attractive seared look, cook the meat directly over the heat source on one side for four minutes, then turn it and finish cooking as the recipe directs.*

| Charcoal | Indirect<br>Searing (optional) see page 6 |
|---|---|
| Gas | Indirect/Medium Heat<br>Searing (optional) see page 6 |
| Grilling time | 35–40 minutes |

| | |
|---|---|
| 6 | large cloves garlic, minced or pressed |
| 1 | tablespoon *each* cumin seeds and chili powder |
| 2 | teaspoons dried oregano |
| 1 | boneless beef triangle tip (tri-tip) or top round roast, about 2¼ pounds (1.02 kg), trimmed of fat |
| 1½ | cups (360 ml) long-grain white rice |
| 1 | tablespoon olive oil or salad oil |
| 1 | medium-size onion, chopped |
| 2 | cans, about 15 ounces (425 g) *each,* black beans |
| ¼ | to ½ teaspoon crushed red pepper flakes |
| ¾ | cup (180 ml) mild salsa, homemade or purchased |
| | Salt and pepper |

Lowfat

Combine 5 of the garlic cloves, cumin, chili powder, and oregano in a small bowl. Pat mixture all over meat, pressing into surface.

Arrange meat in center of cooking grate. Place lid on grill. Cook until an instant-read thermometer inserted in center of thickest part registers 145°F (63°C) for medium-rare (35 to 40 minutes).

Meanwhile, bring 3½ cups (830 ml) water to a boil in a 2- to 3-quart (1.9- to 2.8-liter) pan over high heat. Add rice; reduce heat, cover, and simmer until liquid is absorbed and rice is tender to bite (about 20 minutes). Meanwhile, heat oil in a wide frying pan over medium-high heat. Add onion and remaining garlic. Cook, stirring often, until onion begins to brown (8 to 10 minutes). Add beans and their liquid and red pepper flakes to taste. Bring to a boil; reduce heat and simmer, uncovered, for about 10 minutes.

Stir salsa into rice. Place meat on a board with a well. Slice meat thinly across grain and arrange on a platter or individual plates with rice and beans. Spoon accumulated meat juices over meat. Season to taste with salt and pepper.

MAKES 6 SERVINGS.

*Per serving:* 527 calories (14% from fat), 8 g total fat (2 g saturated fat), 81 mg cholesterol, 941 mg sodium, 68 g carbohydrates, 6 g fiber, 43 g protein, 102 mg calcium, 9 mg iron

# Steak with Classic Peppercorn Sauce

*Flaming brandy and a delectable sauce of mustard, cream, beef broth, and pan juices give this sirloin steak a classy finish.*

| | |
|---|---|
| **Charcoal** | Direct |
| **Gas** | Indirect/Medium Heat Searing (optional) see page 6 |
| **Grilling time** | 14–16 minutes |

½ cup (120 ml) minced shallots

1 teaspoon minced fresh tarragon or ½ teaspoon dried tarragon

¼ cup (60 ml) sherry or balsamic vinegar

1 tablespoon canned green peppercorns, drained and rinsed

1 tablespoon Dijon mustard

3 tablespoons whipping cream

¾ cup (180 ml) beef broth

1 beef sirloin steak, about 1½ pounds (680 g), cut about 1½ inches (3.5 cm) thick; or 1 flank steak, about 1½ pounds (680 g), trimmed of fat

2 tablespoons brandy, warmed (optional)

Salt

Combine shallots, tarragon, vinegar, and ¼ cup (60 ml) water in a wide frying pan. Cook over medium-high heat, stirring often, until liquid has evaporated and browned bits stick to pan. Add 2 tablespoons water and stir to free browned bits. Cook until browned bits begin to accumulate again. Deglaze with 2 more tablespoons water if you want more brown color in sauce. Add peppercorns, mustard, cream, and broth. Cook, stirring often, until reduced to ⅔ cup (160 ml). Set aside

Arrange steak on cooking grate. Place lid on grill. Cook, turning once halfway through cooking time, until meat is done to your liking (for medium-rare: 14 to 16 minutes for sirloin steak; 12 to 15 minutes for flank steak; cut to test). Transfer to a platter and keep warm.

If desired, pour brandy into a long-handled metal cup; set aflame and pour over meat. Shake platter until flame dies (take care meat is *not* beneath an exhaust fan or flammable items). Drain juices from platter into frying pan with sauce. Cook over medium-high heat, stirring, until hot. Slice meat thinly across grain. Spoon sauce over meat. Season to taste with salt.

Makes 6 servings.

*Per serving:* 207 calories (39% from fat), 9 g total fat (4 g saturated fat), 84 mg cholesterol, 327 mg sodium, 4 g carbohydrates, 0 g fiber, 27 g protein, 26 mg calcium, 3 mg iron

# Orange-Coriander Steak

*A portion of the sprightly orange-coriander marinade*
*is simmered to make a fragrant sauce for spooning onto individual servings of the meat.*

| Charcoal | Direct |
|---|---|
| Gas | Indirect/Medium Heat<br>Searing (optional) see page 6 |
| Marinating time | 4 hours or until next day |
| Grilling time | 10–12 minutes |

1    teaspoon grated orange zest

¾    cup (180 ml) orange juice

1    medium-size onion, minced

3    cloves garlic, minced or
     pressed

¼    cup (60 ml) white wine
     vinegar

1½   tablespoons ground coriander

1    teaspoon *each* cracked
     pepper and dried basil

1    lean top round steak, about
     1½ pounds (680 g), cut
     about 1 inch (2.5 cm) thick,
     trimmed of fat

     Finely shredded orange zest

Combine grated orange zest, orange juice, onion, garlic, vinegar, coriander, pepper, and basil in a small bowl. Measure out ½ cup (120 ml) of the marinade; cover and refrigerate.

Place steak in a large heavy-duty plastic food bag or nonreactive bowl. Add remaining marinade and seal bag (or cover bowl). Rotate bag to distribute marinade and place in a shallow pan. Refrigerate for at least 4 hours or until the next day, turning meat occasionally.

Remove steak and drain, reserving marinade. Arrange steak on cooking grate. Place lid on grill. Cook, turning and brushing once with marinade from bag halfway through cooking time, until meat is done to your liking (10 to 12 minutes for medium-rare; cut to test). Meanwhile, bring reserved ½ cup (120 ml) marinade to a boil in a small pan over medium-high heat; remove from heat and keep warm.

Slice steak thinly across grain and arrange on a platter. Garnish with shredded orange zest. Spoon warm sauce over meat.

MAKES 6 SERVINGS.

*Per serving:* 185 calories (21% from fat), 4 g total fat (1 g saturated fat), 72 mg cholesterol, 54 mg sodium, 7 g carbohydrates, 1 g fiber, 28 g protein, 27 mg calcium, 3 mg iron

# Skewered Skirt Steak

*Strips of skirt steak are rippled onto metal skewers, then interlaced with sprigs of fresh herbs, which lend drama to the presentation while also boosting the flavor.*

| | |
|---|---|
| **Charcoal** | Direct |
| **Gas** | Indirect/Medium Heat Searing (optional) see page 6 |
| **Marinating time** | 1 hour or until next day |
| **Grilling time** | 7–9 minutes |

1   tablespoon *each* lemon juice and olive oil

⅓   cup (80 ml) dry red wine

1½   pounds (680 g) skirt steak, trimmed of fat, cut cross-wise into 6 equal pieces

3   small bell peppers (1 *each* red, yellow, and green bell peppers), seeded and cut into sixths

About 12 rosemary sprigs, *each* about 3 inches (8 cm) long

Salt and pepper

## Skirt Steak with Rosemary & Bell Peppers

Combine lemon juice, oil, and wine in a large heavy-duty plastic food bag or nonreactive bowl. Add meat and bell peppers and seal bag (or cover bowl). Rotate bag to distribute marinade and place in a shallow pan. Refrigerate for at least 1 hour or until the next day, turning food occasionally.

Soak rosemary sprigs in water to cover for about 30 minutes. Meanwhile, remove meat and bell peppers from marinade and drain, reserving marinade. Weave 1 piece of meat and 3 bell pepper strips (1 of each color) on each of 6 metal skewers about 15 inches (38 cm) long, rippling meat slightly. Tuck rosemary sprigs between meat and skewer.

Arrange skewers on cooking grate. Place lid on grill. Cook, turning and brushing once with reserved marinade halfway through cooking time, until meat is done to your liking (7 to 9 minutes for medium-rare; cut to test). Season to taste with salt and pepper.

MAKES 6 SERVINGS.

*Per serving:* 294 calories (52% from fat), 16 g total fat (6 g saturated fat), 75 mg cholesterol, 91 mg sodium, 4 g carbohydrates, 1 g fiber, 30 g protein, 18 mg calcium, 3 mg iron

½   cup (120 ml) olive oil

3   tablespoons red wine vinegar

1   tablespoon Dijon mustard

1   clove garlic, minced or pressed

¼   teaspoon pepper

1½   to 2 pounds (680 to 905 g) skirt steak, trimmed of fat, cut crosswise into 12-inch (30-cm) lengths

25   to 30 thyme, rosemary, or tarragon sprigs, *each* about 3 inches (8 cm) long

## Skirt Steak with Fresh Herbs

Combine oil, vinegar, mustard, garlic, and pepper in a large heavy-duty plastic food bag or nonreactive bowl. Add meat and seal bag (or cover bowl). Rotate bag to distribute marinade and place in a shallow pan. Refrigerate for at least 1 hour or until the next day, turning meat occasionally.

Soak herb sprigs in water to cover for about 30 minutes. Meanwhile, remove meat and drain, reserving marinade. Weave each piece of meat onto a metal skewer about 15 inches (38 cm) long, rippling meat slightly. Tuck herb sprigs between meat and skewer.

Arrange skewers on cooking grate. Place lid on grill. Cook, turning and brushing once with reserved marinade halfway through cooking time, until meat is done to your liking (7 to 9 minutes for medium-rare; cut to test).

MAKES 6 TO 8 SERVINGS.

*Per serving:* 259 calories (64% from fat), 18 g total fat (5 g saturated fat), 56 mg cholesterol, 93 mg sodium, 1 g carbohydrates, 0 g fiber, 22 g protein, 18 mg calcium, 3 mg iron

# Flank Steak with Chile-Lime Marinade

*Cracked pepper and a jalapeño chile*
*add the hot notes to this jazzy marinade, while lime zest and juice provide the cooler tones.*

| | |
|---|---|
| **Charcoal** | Direct |
| **Gas** | Indirect/Medium Heat<br>Searing (optional) see page 6 |
| **Marinating time** | 1 hour or until next day |
| **Grilling time** | 12–15 minutes |

¼ cup (60 ml) salad oil

½ teaspoon grated lime zest

⅓ cup (80 ml) lime juice

2 cloves garlic, minced or pressed

1 fresh jalapeño chile, seeded and minced

½ teaspoon cracked pepper

1 flank steak, 1½ to 2 pounds (680 to 905 g), trimmed of fat

**Very Easy**

Combine oil, lime zest, lime juice, garlic, chile, and pepper in a large heavy-duty plastic food bag. Add steak and seal bag securely. Rotate bag to distribute marinade and place in a shallow pan. Refrigerate for at least 1 hour or until the next day, turning bag occasionally.

Remove steak and drain, reserving marinade. Arrange meat on cooking grate. Place lid on grill. Cook, turning and brushing once with reserved marinade halfway through cooking time, until meat is done to your liking (12 to 15 minutes for medium-rare; cut to test). Cut meat across grain into thin, slanting slices.

MAKES 4 TO 6 SERVINGS.

*Per serving:* 300 calories (55% from fat), 18 g total fat (5 g saturated fat), 80 mg cholesterol, 100 mg sodium, 1 g carbohydrates, 0 g fiber, 32 g protein, 11 mg calcium, 3 mg iron

# Flank Steak Italiano

*A pocket stuffed with salami, basil, onion, and provolone cheese makes this Italian-inspired steak a winner.*

| | |
|---|---|
| **Charcoal** | Direct |
| **Gas** | Indirect/Medium Heat Searing (optional) see page 6 |
| **Grilling time** | 12–15 minutes |

1   flank steak, ½ to 2 pounds (680 to 905 g), trimmed of fat

1   tablespoon minced fresh basil or 1 teaspoon dried basil

6   ounces (170 g) thinly sliced dry salami

1   small white onion, thinly sliced

6   ounces (170 g) thinly sliced provolone cheese

**Very Easy**

Lay flank steak flat. With a long, sharp knife, cut a horizontal pocket about three-quarters of the way through meat on a long side. Sprinkle basil evenly inside pocket. Arrange half the salami slices in pocket; top with onion, cheese, and remaining salami. Close opening with 1 or 2 wooden picks.

Arrange steak on cooking grate. Place lid on grill. Cook, turning once halfway through cooking time, until meat is done to your liking (12 to 15 minutes for medium-rare; cut to test). Cut meat across grain into slanting slices about ½ inch (1 cm) thick.

MAKES 4 TO 6 SERVINGS.

*Per serving:* 515 calories (59% from fat), 33 g total fat (15 g saturated fat), 130 mg cholesterol, 1031 mg sodium, 3 g carbohydrates, 0 g fiber, 49 g protein, 279 mg calcium, 4 mg iron

# Carne Asada

*From the tequila in the marinade to the cilantro in the salsa, Mexican flavors abound in this grill-roasted steak (*asada *means "roasted" or "broiled").*
*The steak is cut into thin slices and served in tortillas with salsa and guacamole.*

| | |
|---|---|
| **Charcoal** | Direct |
| **Gas** | Indirect/Medium Heat Searing (optional) see page 6 |
| **Marinating time** | 4 hours or until next day |
| **Grilling time** | 12–15 minutes |

½ cup (120 ml) *each* tequila and orange juice

5 tablespoons lemon juice

3 cloves garlic, minced or pressed

1 medium-size onion, coarsely chopped

½ teaspoon freshly ground pepper

2 pounds (905 g) skirt steak, trimmed of fat

Salsa Bandera (see below)

3 large avocados

¼ teaspoon liquid hot pepper seasoning

Salt

16 flour tortillas, about 7 inches (18 cm) in diameter

## Salsa Bandera

1½ pounds (680 g) tomatoes, chopped

1 tablespoon minced cilantro

2 tablespoons lemon juice

½ cup (120 ml) finely chopped onion

2 or 3 fresh jalapeño chiles, seeded and minced

Salt

Combine tequila, orange juice, 3 tablespoons of the lemon juice, garlic, onion, and pepper in a large heavy-duty plastic food bag. Add meat and seal bag securely. Rotate bag to distribute marinade and place in a shallow pan. Refrigerate for at least 4 hours or until the next day, turning bag occasionally.

Meanwhile, prepare Salsa Bandera by combining tomatoes, cilantro, lemon juice, and onion in a large bowl; add chiles and salt to taste. Cut avocados in half, remove pits, and scoop flesh into another bowl. Coarsely mash. Mix in 1/3 cup (80 ml) of the salsa, remaining lemon juice, and hot pepper seasoning. Season to taste with salt. If made ahead, cover guacamole (press plastic wrap directly onto surface) and salsa separately and refrigerate for up to 4 hours.

Lightly dampen tortillas, stack, and wrap in heavy-duty foil. Remove meat and drain, reserving marinade. Arrange steak and tortilla packet on cooking grate. Place lid on grill. Cook, turning steak and tortillas once halfway through cooking time and brushing steak with remaining marinade, until meat is done to your liking (12 to 15 minutes for medium-rare; cut to test). Thinly slice steak across grain.

To serve, place a few meat slices down center of each tortilla; top with salsa and guacamole. Fold to enclose.

MAKES 6 TO 8 SERVINGS.

*Per serving:* 558 calories (41% from fat), 26 g total fat (7 g saturated fat), 65 mg cholesterol, 404 mg sodium, 49 g carbohydrates, 5 g fiber, 34 g protein, 107 mg calcium, 6 mg iron

**GRILL BY THE BOOK**
**T I P**

Take the precaution of wearing rubber gloves when handling fiery chiles and avoid touching your face or eyes.

# Ginger Pork Chops with Napa Cabbage

*Tender cabbage grills alongside marinated pork chops, and both receive a brushing with a marinade of ginger, sherry, garlic, soy sauce, and sugar that adds just the right hint of sweetness.*

| | |
|---|---|
| **Charcoal** | Direct |
| **Gas** | Indirect/Medium Heat<br>Searing (optional) see page 6 |
| **Marinating time** | 4 hours or until next day |
| **Grilling time** | 10–12 minutes |

¼ cup (60 ml) minced fresh ginger

¾ cup (180 ml) dry sherry

2 cloves garlic, minced or pressed

3 tablespoons soy sauce

2 tablespoons salad oil

1 tablespoon sugar

4 pork shoulder chops, about 1½ pounds (680 g) *total,* cut about ¾ inch (2 cm ) thick, trimmed of fat

2½ pounds (1.15 kg) napa cabbage

Combine ginger, sherry, garlic, soy sauce, oil, and sugar in a large heavy-duty plastic food bag or nonreactive bowl. Add pork chops and seal bag (or cover bowl). Rotate bag to distribute marinade and set in a shallow pan. Refrigerate for at least 4 hours or until the next day, turning chops occasionally. Meanwhile, cut cabbage lengthwise into quarters. Place on a rack over boiling water, cover, and steam just until barely wilted (4 to 5 minutes). If made ahead, let cool; then cover and refrigerate.

Remove chops and drain, reserving marinade. Arrange meat and cabbage on cooking grate. Place lid on grill. Cook, turning and brushing food once with reserved marinade halfway through cooking time, until cabbage is hot and meat near bone is no longer pink (10 to 12 minutes; cut to test). Transfer to a platter or individual plates.

Makes 4 servings.

*Per serving:* 350 calories (54% from fat), 20 g total fat (6 g saturated fat), 89 mg cholesterol, 485 mg sodium, 13 g carbohydrates, 3 g fiber, 25 g protein, 228 mg calcium, 2 mg iron

# Honey-Mustard Ham Steak with Figs

*Skewers of figs accompany a center-cut slice of ham, and a sweet mustard glaze is brushed over both of these grilled offerings.*

| | |
|---|---|
| **Charcoal** | Direct |
| **Gas** | Indirect/Medium Heat |
| **Grilling time** | 8–10 minutes |

2   tablespoons *each* honey
    and Dijon mustard

2   teaspoons cider vinegar

¼   teaspoon coarsely ground
    pepper

16  small or 8 large ripe figs,
    stems trimmed, halved if
    large; or 16 small dried figs

1   center-cut slice, about
    1 pound (455 g), cooked ham

**Very Easy**

Combine honey, mustard, vinegar, and pepper in a small bowl. Thread an equal number of figs on each of 4 skewers.

Arrange figs and ham on cooking grate and brush with some of the honey mixture. Place lid on grill. Cook, turning and brushing once with remaining honey mixture halfway through cooking time, until figs are hot and ham is lightly browned (8 to 10 minutes).

Transfer ham and figs to a platter or individual plates.

MAKES 4 SERVINGS.

*Per serving:* 354 calories (34% from fat), 14 g total fat (5 g saturated fat), 58 mg cholesterol, 1676 mg sodium, 34 g carbohydrates, 3 g fiber, 23 g protein, 54 mg calcium, 1 mg iron

Side dishes, both crisp and creamy, make nice counterpoints to grilled meats. Many such side dishes can be made ahead and refrigerated, a welcome convenience when you want to keep your mind on your grilling. Cabbage dishes keep well. But try to take advantage of fresh seasonal produce as you draw up your menu. That way, you will always have fresh, natural flavors working for you.

## Roast Corn Risotto

| | |
|---|---|
| Charcoal | Direct |
| Gas | Indirect/Medium Heat |
| Grilling time | About 8 minutes |

3   large ears white or yellow corn, husks and silk removed

1   tablespoon olive oil

¼   cup (60 ml) butter or margarine

8   ounces (230 g) mushrooms, thinly sliced

½   cup (120 ml) finely chopped red bell pepper

⅛   teaspoon *each* ground nutmeg and ground white pepper

1   cup (240 ml) chicken broth

Salt

2   tablespoons chopped Italian parsley

Brush corn all over with oil. Arrange on cooking grate. Place lid on grill. Cook, turning once halfway through cooking time, until kernels are streaked with brown and almost tender when pierced (about 8 minutes). Let cool briefly. Cut kernels from cobs, discarding cobs.

In a wide frying pan, melt 2 tablespoons of the butter over medium-high heat. Add mushrooms and cook, stirring often, until most of the liquid has evaporated and mushrooms are lightly browned (about 5 minutes).

Stir in bell pepper, corn, nutmeg, white pepper, and broth. Cook, stirring often, until most of the liquid has evaporated (8 to 10 more minutes). Add remaining butter, stirring until well blended. Season to taste with salt.

Transfer corn mixture to a serving bowl and sprinkle with parsley.

MAKES 4 TO 6 SERVINGS.

*Per serving:* 182 calories (61% calories from fat), 13 g total fat (6 g saturated fat), 25 mg cholesterol, 306 mg sodium, 15 g carbohydrates, 3 g fiber, 4 g protein, 9 mg calcium, 1 mg iron

**Good for a Crowd**

## Cabbage & Ginger Slaw

6   cups (1.4 liters) finely shredded napa cabbage

2   cups (470 ml) shredded carrots

1   large red bell pepper, cut into thin slivers

½   cup (120 ml) *each* finely slivered pickled ginger and seasoned rice vinegar

In a large nonreactive bowl, combine cabbage, carrots, bell pepper, ginger, and vinegar. If made ahead, cover and refrigerate for up to 6 hours.

MAKES 6 SERVINGS.

*Per serving:* 58 calories (4% calories from fat), 0 g total fat (0 g saturated fat), 0 mg cholesterol, 457 mg sodium, 13 g carbohydrates, 2 g fiber, 2 g protein, 74 mg calcium, 1 mg iron

**Lowfat**

## Roasted Tomato Pasta Salad

| | |
|---|---|
| **Charcoal** | Indirect |
| **Gas** | Indirect/Medium Heat |
| **Grilling time** | 35–40 minutes |

Basil Dressing (see below)

10 pear-shaped (Roma-type) tomatoes, cut in half lengthwise

12 ounces (340 g) dried rotini or other spiral-shaped pasta

2 ounces (55 g) string cheese, torn into fine strands

Chopped fresh basil or parsley

Salt

### Basil Dressing

¼ cup (60 ml) finely chopped fresh basil or 2 tablespoons dried basil

½ cup (120 ml) red wine vinegar

¼ cup (60 ml) olive oil

1 tablespoon *each* brown sugar and Dijon mustard

1 clove garlic, minced or pressed

In a small bowl, combine ingredients for Basil Dressing. Pour 3 tablespoons of the dressing into a 9- by 13-inch (23- by 33-cm) foil pan. Add tomatoes, cut side down. Set pan in center of cooking grate. Place lid on grill. Cook until tomatoes are browned at edges (35 to 40 minutes).

Meanwhile, bring 3 quarts (2.8 liters) water to a boil in a 5- to 6-quart (5- to 6-liter) pan over high heat. Stir in pasta, reduce heat to medium-high, and cook just until tender to bite (8 to 10 minutes). Drain, rinse with cold water until cool, and drain again. Pour pasta into a large bowl. Gently stir in ⅔ cup (160 ml) dressing.

Add roasted tomatoes, remaining dressing, and cheese; mix gently. Garnish with chopped basil. Season to taste with salt.

MAKES 4 TO 6 SERVINGS.

*Per serving:* 426 calories (31% calories from fat), 15 g total fat (3 g saturated fat), 6 mg cholesterol, 168 mg sodium, 61 g carbohydrates, 3 g fiber, 13 g protein, 139 mg calcium, 4 mg iron

## Red Slaw

4 cups (950 ml) finely shredded red cabbage

½ cup (120 ml) *each* shredded carrot and chopped red onion

½ cup (120 ml) seasoned rice vinegar; or ½ cup (120 ml) red wine vinegar mixed with 1 tablespoon sugar

1 teaspoon mustard seeds

Salt and pepper

In a large bowl, combine cabbage, carrot, onion, vinegar, and mustard seeds. Season to taste with salt and pepper.

MAKES 6 SERVINGS.

*Per serving:* 41 calories (6% calories from fat), 0 g total fat (0 g saturated fat), 0 mg cholesterol, 406 mg sodium, 9 g carbohydrates, 1 g fiber, 1 g protein, 33 mg calcium, 0 mg iron

Lowfat

# Grilled Pork Chops

*Whether you like them plain, sweetened with a mild citrus glaze, or rubbed with a mixture of spices, pork chops cooked properly on the grill are juicy and nearly irresistible. These are sure to be great family favorites.*

| | |
|---|---|
| **Charcoal** | Indirect<br>Searing (optional) see page 6 |
| **Gas** | Indirect/Medium Heat<br>Searing (optional) see page 6 |
| **Grilling time** | 25–35 minutes |

4   pork center-cut or loin chops, about 2 pounds (905 g) *total*, cut 1¼ to 1½ inches (3 to 3.5 cm) thick, trimmed of fat

Salt and pepper

Very Easy

*Grilled Pork Chops*

### Basic Pork Chops

Season chops to taste with salt and pepper. Arrange in center of cooking grate. Place lid on grill. Cook, turning once halfway through cooking time, until meat near bone is no longer pink (25 to 35 minutes; cut to test).

MAKES 4 SERVINGS.

*Per serving:* 225 calories (38% from fat), 9 g total fat (3 g saturated fat), 91 mg cholesterol, 67 mg sodium, 0 g carbohydrates, 0 g fiber, 34 g protein, 34 mg calcium, 1 mg iron

⅓   cup (80 ml) orange marmalade

2   teaspoons soy sauce

¼   teaspoon ground ginger

Basic Pork Chops
(see above)

### Citrus Pork Chops

Combine marmalade, soy sauce, and ginger in a small bowl. Follow directions for Basic Pork Chops, omitting salt and pepper, and brushing chops with marmalade mixture about 5 minutes before chops are done.

*Per serving:* 292 calories (28% from fat), 9 g total fat (3 g saturated fat), 91 mg cholesterol, 253 mg sodium, 18 g carbohydrates, 0 g fiber, 34 g protein, 45 mg calcium, 1 mg iron

½   teaspoon paprika

¼   teaspoon *each* salt, ground ginger, dried mustard, and pepper

1   clove garlic, minced or pressed

Basic Pork Chops
(see above)

1   tablespoon soy sauce

### Spiced Pork Chops

Combine paprika, salt, ginger, mustard, pepper, and garlic in a small bowl. Follow directions for Basic Pork Chops, brushing chops on both sides with soy sauce and patting paprika mixture all over meat, pressing into surface, before grilling. Do not season with additional salt and pepper.

*Per serving:* 230 calories (37% from fat), 9 g total fat (3 g saturated fat), 91 mg cholesterol, 459 mg sodium, 1 g carbohydrates, 0 g fiber, 34 g protein, 39 mg calcium, 1 mg iron

# Pork on Rye with Relish

*Taking a cue from the classic Reuben, this sandwich features a mustard-coated, boneless pork chop, a mound of tangy cabbage-and-apple relish, and melted fontina cheese on grilled rye.*

| Charcoal | Direct |
|---|---|
| Gas | Indirect/Medium Heat |
| Grilling time | About 7 minutes |

Red Cabbage & Apple Relish
(see below)

8   boneless center-cut pork loin chops, about 1½ pounds (680 g) *total,* cut about ½ inch (1 cm) thick, trimmed of fat

¼   cup (60 ml) coarse-grained mustard

2   tablespoons olive oil

8   slices rye bread

4   ounces (115 g) shredded fontina cheese

## Red Cabbage & Apple Relish

2   tablespoons cider vinegar

1   tablespoon olive oil

2   teaspoons honey

½   teaspoon caraway seeds

1   cup (240 ml) finely shredded red cabbage

½   cup (120 ml) finely chopped Golden Delicious apple

    Salt and pepper

To prepare Red Cabbage & Apple Relish, combine vinegar, oil, honey, caraway seeds, cabbage, and apple in a large bowl. Season to taste with salt and pepper. Cover and refrigerate for up to 4 hours.

Place each chop between 2 sheets of plastic wrap. With a flat-surfaced mallet, pound meat evenly and firmly until about ⅛ inch (3 mm) thick. Coat pork with half the mustard and all the oil. Arrange meat on cooking grate. Place lid on grill. Cook, turning once halfway through cooking time, until meat is no longer pink (about 5 minutes; cut to test). Remove from grill and keep warm.

Place bread on cooler part of cooking grate. Place lid on grill. Cook until bottom is toasted (about 1 minute). Turn bread over, sprinkle 4 of the slices with cheese, and continue to cook until cheese is melted (about 1 more minute).

Set each slice of the plain toast on a dinner plate, spread with remaining mustard, and top with 2 pork chops. Mound with cabbage relish. Arrange cheese-topped bread slices alongside.

MAKES 4 SERVINGS.

*Per serving:* 667 calories (44% from fat), 32 g total fat (11 g saturated fat), 138 mg cholesterol, 878 mg sodium, 40 g carbohydrates, 5 g fiber, 53 g protein, 256 mg calcium, 3 mg iron

# Thai-seasoned Loin Chops with Pesto

*Ice down the beer, because here come some seriously thirst-inducing flavors! This chili paste is easy to make but it imparts a robust taste to the grilled pork. The chops are then served with garlicky cilantro pesto and hot-sweet mustard.*

| | |
|---|---|
| **Charcoal** | Direct |
| **Gas** | Indirect/Medium Heat |
| **Grilling time** | 5–6 minutes |

Thai Chili Paste (see below)

3   cups (710 ml) lightly packed cilantro

1   clove garlic

3   tablespoons olive oil

Salt

8   boneless center-cut pork loin chops, about 1½ pounds (680 g) *total,* cut about 1/2 inch (1 cm) thick, trimmed of fat

½   cup (120 ml) hot-sweet mustard

## Thai Chili Paste

1   teaspoon *each* grated lemon zest and anchovy paste

4   cloves garlic

¼   cup (60 ml) *each* chopped fresh ginger and shallots

1   tablespoon chili powder

½   teaspoon *each* ground coriander, pepper, and crushed red pepper flakes

Combine ingredients for Thai Chili Paste in a blender or food processor. Add 3 tablespoons water and blend until smooth, scraping down sides of container often. If made ahead, cover and refrigerate for up to a day.

Combine cilantro, garlic, and oil in blender. Blend until smooth. Season to taste with salt and set pesto aside.

Spread 1 teaspoon of the chili paste on each side of chops. Place each chop between 2 sheets of plastic wrap. With a flat-surfaced mallet, pound meat evenly and firmly until about 1/4 inch (6 mm) thick. Arrange chops on cooking grate. Place lid on grill. Cook, turning once halfway through cooking time, until meat is no longer pink (5 to 6 minutes; cut to test). Serve with cilantro pesto and mustard.

Makes 4 to 6 servings.

*Per serving:* 351 calories (45% from fat), 17 g total fat (4 g saturated fat), 85 mg cholesterol, 126 mg sodium, 14 g carbohydrates, 1 g fiber, 32 g protein, 62 mg calcium, 2 mg iron

# Lamb Rib Chops with Fresh Peach Chutney

*This winning dish is ready in under 20 minutes. To peel peaches for the chutney,*
*cut a shallow "X" in the end opposite the stem; then*
*dunk the fruit in boiling water for about a minute. The skins will peel off easily.*

| Charcoal | Direct |
|---|---|
| Gas | Indirect/Medium Heat<br>Searing (optional) see page 6 |
| Grilling time | About 10 minutes |

¼    cup (50 g) sugar

¼    cup (60 ml) cider vinegar

1    small onion, minced

½    cup (120 ml) raisins

1    teaspoon *each* ground cinnamon and ground ginger

3    medium-size peaches, peeled, pitted, and sliced about ¼ inch (6 mm) thick

8    to 10 lamb rib chops, 2 to 2¼ pounds (905 g to 1.02 kg) *total,* cut about 1 inch (2.5 cm) thick, trimmed of fat

     Salt and pepper

Lowfat

Combine sugar, vinegar, onion, raisins, cinnamon, and ginger in an 8- to 10-inch (20- to 25-cm) metal-handled pan. Set on cooking grate. Place lid on grill. Cook, stirring occasionally with a long-handled spoon, until onions are soft and raisins are plump (about 5 minutes). Stir in peaches and cook for 3 more minutes. Remove from grill and keep warm.

Arrange chops on cooking grate. Place lid on grill. Cook, turning once halfway through cooking time, until meat is done to your liking (about 10 minutes for medium-rare; cut to test). Serve with peach chutney. Season to taste with salt and pepper.

MAKES 4 SERVINGS.

*Per serving:* 334 calories (27% from fat), 10 g total fat (4 g saturated fat), 70 mg cholesterol, 69 mg sodium, 40 g carbohydrates, 3 g fiber, 23 g protein, 38 mg calcium, 3 mg iron

# Pounded Chops—Lamb, Pork & Veal

*Pounding with a mallet is a time-honored method for tenderizing meat. Here, the pounding serves two other purposes as well: It works in the seasonings and reduces the necessary grilling time.*

| | |
|---|---|
| **Charcoal** | Direct |
| **Gas** | Indirect/Medium Heat |
| **Grilling time** | About 4 minutes |

4    cloves garlic, minced or pressed

2    tablespoons minced fresh rosemary or 1 tablespoon crumbled dried rosemary

½    cup (120 ml) minced parsley

2    tablespoons olive oil or salad oil

4    lamb rib or loin chops, about 1¼ pounds (565 g) *total,* cut about 1 inch (2.5 cm) thick

    Rosemary sprigs

*Pounded Lamb Chops with Rosemary*

## Pounded Lamb Chops with Rosemary

Combine garlic, minced rosemary, parsley, and oil in a small bowl. Slash fat around chops at 1-inch (2.5-cm) intervals. Pat about 1 tablespoon of the rosemary mixture on each side of chops. Place each chop between 2 sheets of plastic wrap. With a flat-surfaced mallet, pound meat evenly and firmly around bone until about ¼ inch (6 mm) thick. (At this point, you may cover and refrigerate chops until the next day.)

Arrange chops on cooking grate. Place lid on grill. Cook, turning once halfway through cooking time, until meat is done to your liking (about 4 minutes for medium-rare; cut to test). Place a chop on each of 4 dinner plates. Garnish with rosemary sprigs.

MAKES 4 SERVINGS.

*Per serving:* 327 calories (78% from fat), 28 g total fat (10 g saturated fat), 71 mg cholesterol, 58 mg sodium, 2 g carbohydrates, 0 g fiber, 16 g protein, 39 mg calcium, 2 mg iron

| Charcoal | Direct |
|---|---|
| Gas | Indirect/Medium Heat |
| Grilling time | 5–6 minutes |

1  tablespoon chili powder

½  teaspoon ground cumin

2  cloves garlic, minced or pressed

1  small onion, minced

2  tablespoons salad oil

4  center-cut pork loin chops, about 1¼ pounds (565 g) *total,* cut about ½ inch (1 cm) thick

2  medium-size avocados

1  small orange, cut into 4 wedges

   Cilantro sprigs

## Pounded Pork & Chili Chops

Combine chili powder, cumin, garlic, onion, and oil in a small bowl. Slash fat around edges of chops at about 1-inch (2.5-cm) intervals. Spread about 1 tablespoon of the chili mixture on each side of chops. Pound as directed for Pounded Lamb Chops with Rosemary (facing page).

Arrange chops on cooking grate. Place lid on grill. Cook, turning once halfway through cooking time, until meat is no longer pink near bone (5 to 6 minutes; cut to test).

Cut avocados in half and remove pits. Place a chop, an avocado half, and an orange wedge on each of 4 dinner plates. Garnish with cilantro.

MAKES 4 SERVINGS.

*Per serving:* 407 calories (65% from fat), 30 g total fat (7 g saturated fat), 63 mg cholesterol, 73 mg sodium, 12 g carbohydrates, 3 g fiber, 25 g protein, 58 mg calcium, 2 mg iron

| Charcoal | Direct |
|---|---|
| Gas | Indirect/Medium Heat |
| Grilling time | 4–5 minutes |

3  tablespoons minced fresh thyme or 1½ tablespoons dried thyme

2  teaspoons grated lemon zest

½  cup (120 ml) minced parsley

2  tablespoons olive oil or salad oil

4  veal rib or loin chops, about 1¼ pounds (565 g) *total,* cut about 1 inch (2.5 cm) thick

   Lemon wedges

## Pounded Veal Chops with Lemon & Thyme

Combine thyme, lemon zest, parsley, and oil in a small bowl. Slash connective tissue around chops at 1-inch (2.5-cm) intervals. Pat about 1 tablespoon of the thyme mixture on each side of chops. Pound as directed for Pounded Lamb Chops with Rosemary (facing page).

Arrange chops on cooking grate. Place lid on grill. Cook, turning once halfway through cooking time, until meat is done to your liking (4 to 5 minutes for medium; cut to test). Place a chop on each of 4 dinner plates. Garnish with lemon wedges.

MAKES 4 SERVINGS.

*Per serving:* 238 calories (66% from fat), 17 g total fat (5 g saturated fat), 82 mg cholesterol, 73 mg sodium, 2 g carbohydrates, 0 g fiber, 18 g protein, 50 mg calcium, 3 mg iron

**GRILL BY THE BOOK**
**T I P**

Pounding chops makes them more tender and allows them to cook through more quickly; slashing fat around the edges prevents them from curling.

# Minted Lamb Chops with Pilaf

*The minty marinade used on the lamb also serves as a baste for the skewers of mushrooms.*
*Lemon and olive flavors accent the brown-and-wild-rice pilaf.*

| Charcoal | Direct |
|---|---|
| Gas | Indirect/Medium Heat<br>Searing (optional) see page 6 |
| Marinating time | 30 minutes or until next day |
| Grilling time | About 10 minutes |

Pilaf Salad (see below)

1   teaspoon olive oil

2   tablespoons dry vermouth

½   teaspoon pepper

¼   cup (60 ml) coarsely
    chopped fresh mint

4   lamb loin chops, about
    1½ pounds (680 g) *total,* cut
    about 1 inch (2.5 cm) thick,
    trimmed of fat

16  medium-large mushrooms

    Salt

4   cherry tomatoes

    Mint sprigs

## Pilaf Salad

½   cup (120 ml) wild rice, rinsed
    and drained

1¾  cups (420 ml) chicken broth

¾   cup (180 ml) long-grain
    brown rice

    About 3 tablespoons lemon
    juice

¼   cup (60 ml) sliced ripe olives

⅓   cup (80 ml) plain nonfat
    yogurt

1   cup (240 ml) halved cherry
    tomatoes

    Salt

To prepare Pilaf Salad, combine wild rice, broth, and 1 cup (240 ml) water in a 2- to 3-quart (1.9- to 2.8-liter) pan. Bring to a boil over high heat. Reduce heat, cover, and simmer for 20 minutes. Add brown rice and continue to cook, covered, until rices are tender to bite (about 25 more minutes). Remove from heat and, with a fork, stir in 3 tablespoons of the lemon juice and olives. Cover and refrigerate until cool (about 45 minutes) or until the next day.

Meanwhile, combine oil, vermouth, pepper, and chopped mint in a large heavy-duty plastic food bag or nonreactive bowl. Add chops and seal bag (or cover bowl). Rotate bag to distribute marinade and place in a shallow pan. Refrigerate for at least 30 minutes or until the next day, turning chops occasionally.

Thread mushrooms through caps onto skewers. Remove chops and drain, reserving marinade. Brush mushrooms with some of the reserved marinade. Arrange chops and mushrooms on cooking grate. Place lid on grill. Cook, turning and brushing food once with reserved marinade halfway through cooking time, until mushrooms and chops are browned and meat is still pink in center (about 10 minutes for medium-rare; cut to test).

Transfer to a platter. Season to taste with salt. With a fork, stir yogurt and cherry tomato halves into pilaf and season to taste with salt and more lemon juice; arrange on platter. Garnish with tomatoes and mint sprigs.

MAKES 4 SERVINGS.

*Per serving:* 427 calories (23% from fat), 11 g total fat (3 g saturated fat), 62 mg cholesterol, 595 mg sodium, 53 g carbohydrates, 5 g fiber, 30 g protein, 82 mg calcium, 4 mg iron

# Lamb Chops with Blue Cheese Pockets

*A marinade of soy sauce, brown sugar, onion, lemon, and garlic lightly caramelizes on the surface of grilled lamb chops that have been stuffed with a nutty cheese filling.*

| Charcoal | Direct |
|---|---|
| Gas | Indirect/Medium Heat Searing (optional) see page 6 |
| Marinating time | 30 minutes–6 hours |
| Grilling time | About 10 minutes |

8   small lamb rib chops, about 2 pounds (905 g) *total,* cut about 1 inch (2.5 cm) thick, trimmed of fat

½   small onion, cut into chunks

¼   cup (60 ml) soy sauce

2   tablespoons *each* firmly packed brown sugar and lemon juice

1   large clove garlic

⅓   cup (80 ml) pine nuts or slivered almonds

⅓   cup (80 ml) crumbled blue-veined cheese

    Pepper

With a sharp knife, cut a horizontal pocket 1½ inches (3.5 cm) wide in each chop, from meaty side to bone.

In a blender or food processor, whirl onion, soy sauce, sugar, lemon juice, and garlic until smooth. Pour into a large heavy-duty plastic food bag. Add chops and seal bag securely. Rotate bag to distribute marinade and place in a shallow pan. Refrigerate for at least 30 minutes or up to 6 hours, turning bag occasionally.

Meanwhile, toast pine nuts in a small frying pan over medium heat, shaking pan often, until golden (3 to 5 minutes). Transfer nuts to a small bowl and stir in blue cheese; season to taste with pepper.

Remove chops and drain, reserving marinade. Using a spoon, stuff cheese filling deep into pocket of each chop. Arrange chops on cooking grate. Place lid on grill. Cook, turning and brushing once with reserved marinade halfway through cooking time, until meat is done to your liking (about 10 minutes for medium-rare; cut to test).

Makes 4 servings.

*Per serving:* 318 calories (53% from fat), 19 g total fat (6 g saturated fat), 74 mg cholesterol, 1251 mg sodium, 13 g carbohydrates, 2 g fiber, 27 g protein, 89 mg calcium, 3 mg iron

# Stuffed Veal Loin Chops

*Prosciutto, fontina cheese, and sage make a tasty filling for these veal loin chops. For an elegant dinner that's quick to prepare, accompany the chops with grilled squash and a simple rice pilaf or risotto.*

| Charcoal | Direct |
|---|---|
| Gas | Indirect/Medium Heat<br>Searing (optional) see page 6 |
| Grilling time | 12–14 minutes |

4    veal loin chops, about 2 pounds (905 g) *total*, cut about 1 inch (2.5 cm) thick, trimmed of fat

2    ounces (55 g) thinly sliced prosciutto

4    slices, about 1 ounce (30 g) *each*, fontina cheese

4    teaspoons minced fresh sage or 1 teaspoon dried sage

2    teaspoons olive oil

2    teaspoons balsamic or red wine vinegar

    Freshly ground pepper

    Sage leaves

Very Easy

With a sharp knife, cut a horizontal slit about 1½ inches (3.5 cm) wide in each chop from meaty side to bone; widen slit near bone. Stuff a quarter of the prosciutto and 1 slice of the cheese deep into pocket of each chop. Sprinkle a quarter of the minced sage inside each pocket.

Combine oil and vinegar in a small bowl. Brush all over chops; sprinkle lightly with pepper. Arrange chops on cooking grate. Place lid on grill. Cook, turning once halfway through cooking time, until meat is done to your liking (12 to 14 minutes for medium; cut to test). Transfer to a platter or individual plates. Garnish with sage leaves.

MAKES 4 SERVINGS.

*Per serving:* 346 calories (54% from fat), 20 g total fat 9 g saturated fat), 155 mg cholesterol, 589 mg sodium, 1 g carbohydrates, 0 g fiber, 39 g protein, 181 mg calcium, 1 mg iron

# Veal Rib Chops with White Beans & Fennel

*This Tuscan-inspired dish makes a memorable meal served with a crisp green salad and a glass of red wine. To make quick work of the Parmesan shavings, use a vegetable peeler to scrape curls of cheese from a wedge of Parmesan.*

| Charcoal | Direct |
|---|---|
| Gas | Indirect/Medium Heat<br>Searing (optional) see page 6 |
| Grilling time | 10–14 minutes |

1   large head fennel, with green feathery leaves attached

2   tablespoons olive oil

1   large clove garlic, minced or pressed

1   cup (240 ml) chopped fresh tomatoes or canned tomatoes and their liquid

1   teaspoon dried thyme

⅛   to ¼ teaspoon crushed red pepper flakes

2   cans, about 15 ounces (425 g) *each,* white beans, drained

6   veal rib chops, about 1¾ pounds (795 g) *total,* cut ¾ (2 cm) thick, trimmed of fat

2   ounces (55 g) thinly shaved Parmesan cheese

Trim coarse stems and root end from fennel. Pull green feathery leaves from stems; reserve 6 sprigs. Mince remaining leaves and set aside. Cut bulbs in half lengthwise and thinly slice crosswise.

Heat 1 tablespoon of the oil and garlic in a wide frying pan over medium-high heat. Add sliced fennel. Cook, stirring often, until fennel begins to brown (about 8 minutes). Stir in tomatoes, ½ teaspoon of the thyme, red pepper flakes to taste, and beans. Cook, stirring occasionally, until some of liquid has evaporated and mixture is slightly thickened (7 to 10 minutes). Stir in minced fennel leaves; remove from heat and keep warm.

Combine remaining oil and thyme in a small bowl; brush over veal. Arrange chops on cooking grate. Place lid on grill. Cook, turning once halfway through cooking time, until meat is done to your liking (10 to 14 minutes for medium; cut to test).

Spoon bean mixture onto 6 dinner plates. Place chops on beans and sprinkle with Parmesan. Garnish with reserved fennel leaves.

MAKES 6 SERVINGS.

*Per serving:* 292 calories (40% from fat), 13 g total fat (4 g saturated fat), 80 mg cholesterol, 537 mg sodium, 17 g carbohydrates, 5 g fiber, 26 g protein, 206 mg calcium, 3 mg iron

# Classic Bacon Cheeseburgers

*Some tried-and-true diner recipes are very hard to beat. But these fast-food classics taste even better when grilled at home with the freshest possible ingredients.*

| | |
|---|---|
| Charcoal | Direct |
| Gas | Indirect/Medium Heat Searing (optional) see page 6 |
| Grilling time | About 10 minutes |

12 ounces (340 g) extra-thick sliced bacon

1 medium-size red onion, cut into 6 slices, *each* about ¼ inch (6 mm) thick

2 pounds (905 g) lean top round, freshly ground

Salt and pepper

6 thin slices, about 1 ounce (30 g) *each*, extra-sharp Cheddar cheese

6 hamburger buns, split and toasted

Cook bacon in a wide frying pan over medium heat until crisp (8 to 10 minutes). Remove and drain on paper towels; set aside. Discard all but 1 tablespoon of the drippings. Lay onion slices in pan, turning to coat in drippings. Remove pan from heat.

Shape meat into 6 patties, each about ¾ inch (2 cm) thick. Season to taste with salt and pepper. Arrange patties and onion slices on cooking grate. Place lid on grill. Cook, turning meat and onion once halfway through cooking time (about 10 minutes for medium; cut to test). Top patties with cheese.

Transfer patties to hamburger buns; top with onion and bacon.

MAKES 6 SERVINGS.

*Per serving:* 560 calories (44% from fat), 27 g total fat (12 g saturated fat), 140 mg cholesterol, 753 mg sodium, 25 g carbohydrates, 1 g fiber, 52 g protein, 281 mg calcium, 5 mg iron

## Internal Temperatures for Safe Cooking

*The USDA recommendation is that ground meat be cooked to 160°F (71°C) in center of patties or until no longer pink and the juices run clear. Ground poultry should be cooked to 165°F (74°C).*

## Grilling for a Crowd

*Barbecued meats are especially easy entrées to serve when you're entertaining a large group of people. You can usually double or triple the amount of steaks, chops, or burgers called for in a recipe; cooking times remain the same regardless of the number of servings you're grilling.*

*Here are some additional hints:*

■ *Select salads, condiments, breads, and desserts that can be prepared in advance.*

■ *Make a schedule for the foods you're grilling and those you're doing on the stovetop. Working backward from your serving time, decide when to start cooking each dish, so those that cook the longest can be started first.*

■ *Set plates, utensils, and glasses on the table ahead of time.*

■ *Make a list of every food item you're serving so you won't forget something stored in the refrigerator or freezer.*

■ *Enlist help from your guests—and have a great time!*

# Johnny Appleseed Burgers

*Green apples add tart-sweet flavor to these burgers of ground turkey and sausage and to the crisp cabbage slaw that accompanies them.*

| | |
|---|---|
| **Charcoal** | Direct |
| **Gas** | Indirect/Medium Heat<br>Searing (optional) see page 6 |
| **Grilling time** | 10–12 minutes |

Apple Cabbage Slaw
(see below)

1   pound (455 g) lean ground turkey

4   ounces (115 g) lean ground pork sausage

1   egg white

¼   cup (60 ml) *each* fine dried bread crumbs and minced onion

½   cup (120 ml) peeled and finely chopped tart green apple

1   tablespoon minced fresh ginger

4   hamburger buns, split and toasted

Salt

**Apple Cabbage Slaw**

1   cup (240 ml) *each* finely shredded red cabbage and thinly sliced unpeeled tart green apple

3   tablespoons orange juice

1   tablespoon balsamic or red wine vinegar

Combine ingredients for Apple Cabbage Slaw in a large bowl. If made ahead, cover and refrigerate for up to 4 hours.

Combine turkey, pork sausage, egg white, bread crumbs, onion, apple, and ginger in another large bowl. Shape mixture into 4 patties, each about ¾ inch (2 cm) thick. Arrange patties on cooking grate. Place lid on grill. Cook, turning once halfway through cooking time (10 to 12 minutes for medium-well; cut to test).

Transfer patties to hamburger buns and top with slaw. Season to taste with salt.

MAKES 4 SERVINGS.

*Per serving:* 433 calories (37% from fat), 18 g total fat (5 g saturated fat), 65 mg cholesterol, 545 mg sodium, 37 g carbohydrates, 2 g fiber, 31 g protein, 111 mg calcium, 4 mg iron

# Curried Turkey Burgers

*These satisfying turkey burgers, seasoned with curry powder and topped with melted cheese are all the more delicious when you crown them with slices of juicy, ripe tomato.*

| Charcoal | Direct |
|---|---|
| Gas | Indirect/Medium Heat Searing (optional) see page 6 |
| Grilling time | 10–12 minutes |

| | |
|---|---|
| ½ | cup (120 ml) reduced-fat mayonnaise |
| 1½ | tablespoons curry powder |
| 2 | pounds (905 g) lean ground turkey |
| 1 | large onion, minced |
| 1 | egg white |
| 4 | ounces (115 g) jack cheese, thinly sliced |
| 6 | hamburger buns, split and toasted |
| | Salt and pepper |

**Very Easy**

Combine mayonnaise and 1½ teaspoons of the curry powder in a small bowl. Cover and refrigerate until ready to use or for up to 2 days.

In a large bowl, combine turkey with remaining curry powder, onion, and egg white. Shape into 6 equal-size patties, each about ¾ inch (2 cm) thick. Arrange patties on cooking grate. Place lid on grill. Cook, turning once halfway through cooking time (10 to 12 minutes for medium-well; cut to test). Top with cheese.

Spread buns with mayonnaise mixture; top with patties. Season to taste with salt and pepper.

MAKES 6 SERVINGS.

*Per serving:* 522 calories (48% from fat), 27 g total fat (9 g saturated fat), 96 mg cholesterol, 605 mg sodium, 30 g carbohydrates, 2 g fiber, 36 g protein, 244 mg calcium, 4 mg iron

# Fresh Condiments for Grilled Meats

A perfectly grilled steak, a sizzling chop, or a plump, juicy burger gets even better when you dollop on a homemade sauce that captures the best flavors of summer's produce. The toppings presented here are as delicious as they are versatile—and they offer a welcome change of pace from the more familiar steak sauce, catsup, and pickle relish. The vegetable relish and the chile sauce can also be enjoyed as dips served with raw vegetables or chips, while the main course is on the grill.

## Blackberry Catsup

| | |
|---|---|
| 8 | cups (1.9 liters) blackberries, rinsed and drained |
| 1¾ | cups (420 ml) red wine vinegar |
| 1 | cup (240 ml) firmly packed brown sugar |
| 1 | cup (200 g) granulated sugar |
| 2 | teaspoons ground cinnamon |
| 1½ | teaspoons ground allspice |
| 1 | teaspoon ground ginger |
| ½ | teaspoon black pepper |
| ¼ | teaspoon ground red pepper (cayenne) |

In a 4- to 5-quart (4- to 5-liter) pan, cook berries over medium-high heat, stirring often, until berries get juicy and begin to fall apart (about 10 minutes). Rub berries and juice through a fine strainer into a bowl; discard seeds.

Return berry juice to pan and add vinegar, brown sugar, granulated sugar, cinnamon, allspice, ginger, black pepper, and ground red pepper. Bring to a boil over high heat; reduce heat and simmer, stirring often, until mixture is reduced to about 2½ cups (590 ml), about 1 hour. Let cool. If made ahead, cover and refrigerate for up to 2 weeks.

MAKES ABOUT 2½ CUPS (590 ML).

*Per tablespoon:* 58 calories (2% calories from fat), 0 g total fat (0 g saturated fat), 0 mg cholesterol, 2 mg sodium, 14 g carbohydrates, 1 g fiber, 1 g protein, 16 mg calcium, 1 mg iron

## Summer Harvest Catsup

| | |
|---|---|
| 6 | pounds (2.7 kg) pear-shaped (Roma-type) tomatoes, chopped |
| 1 | large onion, chopped |
| 2 | tablespoons chopped garlic |
| 1½ | cups (360 ml) cider vinegar |
| 1 | cup (200g) sugar |
| 1 | teaspoon ground coriander |
| ½ | to ¾ teaspoon ground red pepper (cayenne) |
| ½ | teaspoon ground mace or ground nutmeg |
| ¼ | teaspoon ground cinnamon |
| 1 | bayleaf |
| | About 1¼ teaspoons salt |

In a blender or food processor, combine tomatoes, onion, and garlic, a portion at a time, and blend until smoothly puréed. Pour tomato mixture through a fine strainer placed over a 5- to 6-quart (5- to 6-liter) pan, stirring and pressing to push mixture through. Discard residue left in strainer.

Add vinegar, sugar, coriander, red pepper, mace, cinnamon, and bay leaf to mixture in pan. Bring to a boil over medium-high heat and cook, stirring, until reduced to about 4 cups (950 ml), 1½ to 2 hours; adjust heat to maintain a gentle boil, lowering heat if mixture splatters out of pan.

Add salt to taste. Remove and discard bay leaf. If made ahead, let cool; then cover and refrigerate for up to 1 month.

MAKES ABOUT 1 QUART (950 ML).

*Per tablespoon:* 24 calories (5% calories from fat), 0 g total fat (0 g saturated fat), 0 mg cholesterol, 47 mg sodium, 6 g carbohydrates, 1 g fiber, 0 g protein, 4 mg calcium, 0 mg iron

### Hot & Spicy Chile Sauce

| | |
|---|---|
| 2 | to 2½ pounds (905 g to 1.15 kg) tomatoes |
| ⅔ | cup (160 ml) cider vinegar |
| ½ | cup (120 ml) chopped onion |
| 6 | tablespoons sugar |
| ½ | teaspoon *each* mustard seeds, salt, and crushed red pepper flakes |
| ¼ | teaspoon *each* ground ginger and ground nutmeg |
| ⅛ | teaspoon curry powder |

Peel and coarsely chop the tomatoes, you should have about 1 quart (950 ml).

In a 3½- to 4-quart (3.3- to 4-liter) pan, combine tomatoes, vinegar, onion, sugar, mustard seeds, salt, red pepper flakes, ginger, nutmeg, and curry powder. Bring to a boil over medium-high heat; reduce heat and simmer, stirring occasionally, until mixture is reduced to about 2 cups (470 ml), about 1½ hours; as mixture thickens, stir often to prevent sticking.

Let cool. If made ahead, cover and refrigerate for up to 1 month.

MAKES ABOUT 2 CUPS (470 ML).

*Per tablespoon:* 17 calories (5% calories from fat), 0 g total fat (0 g saturated fat), 0 mg cholesterol, 37 mg sodium, 4 g carbohydrates, 0 g fiber, 0 g protein, 3 mg calcium, 0 mg iron

---

### Tangy Horseradish-Chive Mayonnaise

| | |
|---|---|
| ⅓ | cup (80 ml) *each* mayonnaise and plain low-fat yogurt |
| 1 | tablespoon *each* Dijon mustard, prepared horseradish, and finely chopped chives |

In a small bowl, combine mayonnaise, yogurt, mustard, horseradish, and chives.

MAKES ABOUT ¾ CUP (180 ML).

*Per tablespoon:* 49 calories (91% calories from fat), 5 g total fat (1 g saturated fat), 4 mg cholesterol, 70 mg sodium, 0 g carbohydrates, 0 g fiber, 0 g protein, 13 mg calcium, 0 mg iron

---

### Grilled Zucchini & Tomato Relish

| Charcoal | Direct |
|---|---|
| Gas | Indirect/Medium Heat |
| Grilling time | 45-60 minutes |

| | |
|---|---|
| 4 | medium-size pear-shaped (Roma-type) tomatoes, halved |
| 2 | medium-size zucchini, sliced about 1 inch (2.5 cm) thick |
| 1 | medium-size red onion, cut into 8 wedges |
| 6 | cloves garlic, crushed |
| 1 | tablespoon olive oil |
| 2 | tablespoons chopped parsley |
| | Salt |

In a 9- by 13-inch (23- by 33-cm) foil pan, combine tomatoes, zucchini, onion, garlic, and oil. Set pan on cooking grate. Place lid on grill. Cook for 20 minutes. Using a wide metal spatula, turn vegetables; remove garlic and set aside. Continue to cook until tomatoes are tender when pressed (20 to 25 more minutes).

Let vegetables cool briefly; then coarsely chop vegetables and garlic. Transfer to a serving bowl and stir in parsley. Season to taste with salt. Serve warm or at room temperature.

MAKES ABOUT 2½ CUPS (590 ML).

*Per tablespoon:* 9 calories (37% calories from fat), 0 g total fat (0 g saturated fat), 0 mg cholesterol, 2 mg sodium, 1 g carbohydrates, 1 g fiber, 0 g protein, 4 mg calcium, 0 mg iron

# Chicken Burgers with Basil & Dried Tomatoes

*These chicken burgers are terrific on Italian flat bread (focaccia) or on sourdough French bread. The flavorings—red onion, basil, sun-dried tomatoes, and garlic—go in the burgers to give them plenty of taste. Look for focaccia in Italian delicatessens, bakeries or well-stocked markets.*

| Charcoal | Direct |
| --- | --- |
| Gas | Indirect/Medium Heat<br>Searing (optional) see page 6 |
| Grilling time | 10–12 minutes |

2  tablespoons balsamic or red wine vinegar

1  tablespoon olive oil

¼  teaspoon *each* salt and pepper

2  pounds (905 g) lean ground chicken

1  egg white

1  medium-size red onion, finely chopped

½  cup (120 ml) minced fresh basil or 2 tablespoons dried basil

⅓  cup (80 ml) drained and minced sun-dried tomatoes in olive oil

2  cloves garlic, minced or pressed

1  pound (455 g) plain focaccia, cut into 6 equal-size pieces, split horizontally, and toasted; or sourdough French bread, sliced and toasted

   Mayonnaise (optional)

   Arugula leaves or other salad greens, rinsed and crisped

Combine vinegar, oil, salt, and pepper in a small bowl; set aside.

In a large bowl, combine chicken, egg white, onion, basil, tomatoes, and garlic. Shape into 6 equal-size patties, each about ¾ inch (2 cm) thick. Arrange patties on cooking grate. Place lid on grill. Cook, turning once halfway through cooking time (10 to 12 minutes for medium-well; cut to test).

Brush cut sides of focaccia with oil mixture; spread with mayonnaise, if desired. Place patties on bread and top with arugula and another piece of focaccia.

MAKES 6 SERVINGS.

*Per serving:* 556 calories (45% from fat), 28 g total fat (7 g saturated fat), 189 mg cholesterol, 567 mg sodium, 40 g carbohydrates, 3 g fiber, 37 g protein, 208 mg calcium, 4 mg iron

# Pizza Burgers

*Parmesan, herbs, provolone, and pizza sauce transform one kids' favorite
into another altogether.*

| Charcoal | Direct |
|---|---|
| Gas | Indirect/Medium Heat Searing (optional) see page 6 |
| Grilling time | About 11 minutes |

1   pound (455 g) lean ground beef

1   egg

3   ounces (85 g) grated Parmesan cheese

¼   cup (60 ml) minced parsley

1   small onion, finely chopped

¾   teaspoon *each* dried basil, dried oregano, dried rosemary, and pepper

¼   teaspoon fennel seeds

4   slices, about 4 ounces (115 g) *total,* provolone cheese

4   English muffins, split

¼   to ½ cup (60 to 120 ml) prepared pizza sauce or spaghetti sauce

Combine meat, egg, Parmesan, parsley, onion, basil, oregano, rosemary,
pepper, and fennel in a large bowl. Shape mixture into 4 patties, each about
¾ inch (2 cm) thick.

    Arrange patties on cooking grate. Place lid on grill. Cook, turning once
halfway through cooking time (about 10 minutes for medium; cut to test).
Top each patty with a slice of provolone and lay muffins, cut side down, on
cooking grate. Continue to cook until cheese is melted (about 1 more
minute).

    Transfer patties to muffins. Serve with pizza sauce.

MAKES 4 SERVINGS.

*Per serving:* 565 calories (48% from fat), 30 g total fat (14 g saturated fat), 155 mg cholesterol, 969 mg sodium,
32 g carbohydrates, 2 g fiber, 40 g protein, 560 mg calcium, 4 mg iron

# International Burgers

*When ordinary burgers simply won't do, here are three wonderful ways to extend your repertoire.*

| Charcoal | Direct |
|---|---|
| Gas | Indirect/Medium Heat<br>Searing (optional) see page 6 |
| Grilling time | About 10 minutes |

| | |
|---|---|
| 1 | pound (455 g) mild Italian sausages |
| ¼ | cup (60 ml) dried bread crumbs |
| 1 | small onion, finely chopped |
| 1 | egg, beaten |
| 1½ | teaspoons minced fresh oregano or ½ teaspoon dried oregano |
| 1 | loaf, about 1½ pounds (680 g), French bread, cut into 12 slices, toasted |
| 4 | ounces (115 g) shredded mozzarella cheese |
| 1 | jar, about 6 ounces (170 g), marinated artichoke hearts, drained and thinly sliced through stem |
| ½ | small red onion, thinly sliced |
| 1 | small red bell pepper, seeded and cut into thin strips |

*Curried Lamb Burger in Pita Bread*

**Italian Sausage Burgers**

Remove casings from sausages. Combine sausages, bread crumbs, chopped onion, egg, and oregano in a large bowl. Shape mixture into 6 oblong patties, each about same size as French bread slices.

Arrange patties on cooking grate. Place lid on grill. Cook, turning once halfway through cooking time (about 10 minutes for medium; cut to test).

Transfer patties to bread slices. Top with cheese, artichokes, sliced onion, bell pepper, and remaining bread.

MAKES 6 SERVINGS.

*Per serving:* 616 calories (37% from fat), 25 g total fat (9 g saturated fat), 93 mg cholesterol, 1469 mg sodium, 69 g carbohydrates, 4 g fiber, 28 g protein, 227 mg calcium, 5 mg iron

| | |
|---|---|
| Charcoal | Direct |
| Gas | Indirect/Medium Heat Searing (optional) see page 6 |
| Grilling time | About 10 minutes |

- 1 pound (455 g) lean ground pork
- 1 small onion, finely chopped
- ¼ cup (60 ml) dried bread crumbs
- 1 egg, beaten
- ½ cup (120 ml) finely chopped water chestnuts or celery
- 1 clove garlic, minced or pressed
- 2 tablespoons soy sauce
- 2 teaspoons minced fresh ginger
- 8 flour tortillas, 7 to 9 inches (18 to 23 cm) in diameter

  Hoisin sauce

  Green onions, cut into matchstick-size pieces

  Bean sprouts

  Cilantro sprigs

**Mo Shu Burgers**

Combine pork, chopped onion, bread crumbs, egg, water chestnuts, garlic, soy sauce, and ginger in a large bowl. Shape mixture into 8 equal-size logs, each about 3 inches (8 cm) long.

Lightly dampen tortillas, stack, and wrap in heavy-duty foil. Arrange meat and tortilla packet on cooking grate. Place lid on grill. Cook, turning meat and tortillas once halfway through cooking time (about 10 minutes for medium; cut to test).

Spread hoisin sauce on tortillas. Place a pork log near lower edge of each tortilla; top with onion pieces, bean sprouts, and cilantro. Fold tortilla over filling, turn in sides, and roll to enclose.

MAKES 4 TO 8 SERVINGS.

*Per serving:* 358 calories (38% from fat), 15 g total fat (4 g saturated fat), 95 mg cholesterol, 665 mg sodium, 34 g carbohydrates, 2 g fiber, 21 g protein, 82 mg calcium, 3 mg iron

| | |
|---|---|
| Charcoal | Direct |
| Gas | Indirect/Medium Heat Searing (optional) see page 6 |
| Grilling time | About 10 minutes |

- 1 pound (455 g) lean ground lamb
- 1 small onion, finely chopped
- ¼ cup (60 ml) dried bread crumbs
- ⅓ cup (80 ml) finely chopped dried apricots
- 1 egg, beaten
- 2 teaspoons curry powder
- 3 pita breads, about 6 inches (15 cm) in diameter, cut in half crosswise

  Major Grey's chutney, chopped

  Plain yogurt

  Sliced cucumbers

**Curried Lamb Burgers in Pita Bread**

Combine lamb, onion, bread crumbs, apricots, egg, and curry powder in a large bowl. Shape mixture into 6 oblong patties, each 3 to 4 inches (8 to 10 cm) long.

Wrap pita bread in heavy-duty foil. Arrange patties and bread packet on cooking grate. Place lid on grill. Cook, turning meat and bread once halfway through cooking time (about 10 minutes for medium; cut to test).

Place patties in pita bread halves. Serve with chutney, yogurt, and cucumbers.

MAKES 6 SERVINGS.

*Per serving:* 253 calories (26% from fat), 7 g total fat (2 g saturated fat), 87 mg cholesterol, 257 mg sodium, 26 g carbohydrates, 2 g fiber, 20 g protein, 61 mg calcium, 3 mg iron

# Greek Megaburgers

*This showstopping giant among burgers is presented on a round loaf of bread. The top half is precut to simplify serving.*

| | |
|---|---|
| **Charcoal** | Direct |
| **Gas** | Indirect/Medium Heat Searing (optional) see page 6 |
| **Grilling time** | About 15 minutes |

1   round loaf, about 1½ pounds (680 g), French bread, 10 to 11 inches (25 to 28 cm) in diameter

4   ounces (115 g) butter or margarine, at room temperature

5   cloves garlic, minced or pressed

2   small packages, 3 ounces (85 g) *each,* cream cheese, at room temperature

4   ounces (115 g) feta cheese, crumbled

3   tablespoons lemon juice

1   small onion, finely chopped

2   teaspoons dried oregano

¾   teaspoon ground coriander

1   teaspoon salt

¼   cup (60 ml) *each* minced fresh mint and parsley

1   pound (455 g) *each* lean ground beef and lean ground lamb

1   large red onion, thinly sliced

2   medium-size tomatoes, sliced

1   jar, about 6 ounces (170 g), marinated artichoke hearts, drained

Mint sprig

Good for a Crowd

Using a long serrated knife, cut the bread in half horizontally. In a small bowl, beat butter with 2 cloves of the garlic; spread over cut sides of bread and set aside. In a small bowl, beat cream cheese until smooth; stir in feta cheese. Cover and refrigerate until ready to use.

In a large bowl, combine lemon juice, chopped onion, remaining garlic, oregano, coriander, salt, minced mint, parsley, beef, and lamb. Turn onto a large baking sheet lined with wax paper; pat into a round patty about 1 inch (2.5 cm) wider than bread.

Invert patty onto cooking grate. Place lid on grill. Cook for 7 minutes and turn (using 1 rimless baking sheet as a pusher, slide patty onto a second sheet, hold patty between baking sheets, and invert sheets to flip patty). Cook about 7 more minutes for medium; cut to test.

Slide burger onto a baking sheet; keep warm. Place bread, cut side down, on cooking grate. Place lid on grill. Cook until lightly toasted (about 1 minute). Slide burger onto bottom half of bread. Layer cream cheese mixture, sliced onion, tomatoes, and artichokes on burger. Garnish with mint sprig. Cut into serving-size wedges. Slice top half of bread into wedges and serve with burger.

MAKES 8 TO 10 SERVINGS.

*Per serving:* 610 calories (50% from fat), 34 g total fat (17 g saturated fat), 125 mg cholesterol, 1168 mg sodium, 46 g carbohydrates, 3 g fiber, 30 g protein, 172 mg calcium, 4 mg iron

**GRILL BY THE BOOK**
**T I P**

Use small cookie sheets as giant spatulas to turn oversize burgers like these.

# Walnut, Cheese & Herb Burgers

*Nuts, grains, eggs, and cheese contribute a healthy
dose of protein to these vegetarian burgers. Enjoy them topped with lettuce, sliced tomatoes,
onion, and creamy Thousand Island dressing.*

| Charcoal | Direct |
| --- | --- |
| Gas | Indirect/Medium Heat |
| Grilling time | 9–10 minutes |

2    eggs

⅔    cup (160 ml) soft whole wheat bread crumbs

½    cup (120 ml) *each* chopped walnuts, sliced green onions, toasted wheat germ, and small-curd cottage cheese

2    tablespoons chopped parsley

1    tablespoon fresh minced basil or 1 teaspoon dried basil

1    teaspoon fresh minced oregano or ½ teaspoon dried oregano

½    teaspoon paprika

    Garlic salt

    About 1 tablespoon salad oil

4    slices, 3 ounces (85 g) *total*, jack cheese

    Hamburger buns, split and toasted

Vegetarian

In a large bowl, beat eggs until blended. Stir in bread crumbs, nuts, onions, wheat germ, cottage cheese, parsley, basil, oregano, and paprika. Season to taste with garlic salt. Shape mixture into 4 patties, each about ½ inch (1 cm) thick.

Swirl 1 teaspoon of the oil on a wide metal-handled nonstick griddle. Arrange patties on griddle (2 at a time, if necessary) and set on cooking grate. Place lid on grill. Cook, turning once and adding remaining oil, if needed, halfway through cooking time, until burgers are browned (8 to 9 minutes). Top with jack cheese and cook just until cheese is melted (about 1 more minute). Transfer to hamburger buns.

MAKES 4 SERVINGS.

*Per serving:* 474 calories (50% from fat), 27 g total fat (7 g saturated fat), 133 mg cholesterol, 542 mg sodium, 38 g carbohydrates, 4 g fiber, 23 g protein, 296 mg calcium, 4 mg iron

# Potato-Mushroom Burgers with Chutney

*The Indian heritage of these delicious golden-crusted burgers is evident in the scents of cumin and ginger and in the use of a chutney topping.*

| | |
|---|---|
| **Charcoal** | Direct |
| **Gas** | Indirect/Medium Heat |
| **Grilling time** | About 10 minutes |

- 2 tablespoons butter or margarine
- 1 cup (240 ml) chopped onion
- 2 cloves garlic, minced or pressed
- ½ teaspoon *each* ground cumin and ground ginger
- 1 cup (240 ml) *each* coarsely chopped mushrooms and cooked thin skinned potatoes
- 1 cup (240 ml) diced carrots
- 2 tablespoons chopped cilantro
- ⅓ cup (80 ml) all-purpose flour
- 2 eggs, lightly beaten
- 1 cup (240 ml) soft whole wheat bread crumbs
- Salt and pepper
- About 1 tablespoon salad oil
- ½ cup (120 ml) mango or peach chutney
- 4 hamburger buns, split and toasted

Vegetarian

In a wide frying pan, melt butter over medium heat. Add onion and garlic and cook, stirring, until onion is lightly browned (8 to 10 minutes). Add cumin and ginger; cook, stirring, for 1 more minute. Add mushrooms, potatoes, carrots, and cilantro; cook, stirring, until carrots are tender to bite (about 7 minutes). Add flour and cook, stirring, for 3 more minutes. Remove from heat; let cool briefly. Mix in eggs and bread crumbs. Season to taste with salt and pepper.

Shape mixture into 4 patties, each about ⅓ inch (7 mm) thick. Swirl 1 teaspoon of the oil on a wide metal-handled nonstick griddle. Arrange patties on griddle (2 at a time, if necessary) and set on cooking grate. Place lid on grill. Cook, turning once and adding remaining oil, if needed, halfway through cooking time, until deep golden (about 10 minutes).

Spread patties with chutney and transfer to hamburger buns.

MAKES 4 SERVINGS.

*Per serving:* 461 calories (28% from fat), 15 g total fat (5 g saturated fat), 122 mg cholesterol, 479 mg sodium, 72 g carbohydrates, 4 g fiber, 11 g protein, 120 mg calcium, 4 mg iron

# Index